9.98

Survival Handbook
for
Preschool Parents

Survival Handbook
for
Preschool Parents

Grandparents
Teachers
Nursery School, Day-Care, and
Health Workers

Newly Revised

Dr. Helen Wheeler Smith

ISBN: 0-88290-400-0
Horizon Publishers' Catalog and Order Number: 2051
First Printing: July, 1990

Printing: 1 2 3 4 5 6 7 8 9 10

Printed and distributed
in the United States of America by

Horizon Publishers
& Distributors, Incorporated
P.O. Box 490 Bountiful, Utah 84011-0490

Contents

Preface

This is a small book. I have tried to be brief and to the point because I know busy mothers do not have much time for reading. It contains the knowledge and experience I have gleaned in forty years of trying to find out what makes one child a pleasure and another a problem.

I am indebted to my husband, who has always been a dedicated father to our three daughters and twin sons, and to these children, who have taught me the really important things about being a parent.

Our eight grandchildren have furnished me with an observation laboratory. The effects of different child-raising methods on these children, now two years to twenty-two years old, have helped clarify my insights.

When our oldest daughter entered college, the financial demands of tuition, music lessons, and orthodontic work for five children swamped our budget, so I started to teach in elementary school to stay afloat.

During the next ten years I came to the conclusion that the problems most children had in school had been caused long before they started kindergarten. By this time only our boys were still in college, so I gave up full-time teaching to return to the University of Utah to learn everything I could about Early Childhood Education and started a class for preschool mothers.

I am grateful to the YWCA for its encouragement in setting up my class, Mommy and Me, in 1968. The YW provides the play center for infants and children so the mothers can attend classes. The class is now called How to Parent and is offered twice a year.

Finding answers and solutions to the many problems and frustrations of these young mothers has helped me refine the mass of material available into a useful course for mothers of preschool children.

I have tried to teach a philosophy about children— that a child is a separate person with his or her own potential. When parents so view the child, their practices in rearing that child will work toward such a goal.

For brevity, I have used "he," but I mean all the little girls as well.

> The children of today make
> the world of tomorrow.

Introduction

John Bradshaw in his book *Bradshaw On The Family* has pulled together the recent research from all fields of study to support his premise that, "Nothing has changed in our family practices for a hundred and fifty years and we keep producing more and more people with problems in our society because of our dysfunctional family systems."

The dysfunctional family does not meet the basic dependency needs of its children under eight years old. The parents did not have their own dependency needs met, so they treat their children the way they were treated.

This produces what Bradshaw calls "An Adult Child" whose loss of self as a small child made him feel abandoned so he/she lives his/her life without the Trust, the Self Control and the Will he didn't learn before he/she was eight.

Children view themselves the way they are treated. All of their future choices depend on whether they were made to feel valued and capable, or not valued and incapable.

"These old rules" (do as I say), says Bradshaw, "produce shame in children, because children blame themselves when parents don't accept them, and they totally lack self acceptance."

Shame differs from guilt. Guilt says I've done something wrong; shame says there's something wrong with me. Guilt says I made a mistake; shame says I AM a mistake. Guilt says, what I did was not good; shame says I AM no good.

Parents shame their children by using the following practices:

1. By actually physically leaving them.

2. By not modeling their (parents) own emotions for their children.

3. By not being there to affirm their children's expressions of all the emotions.

4. By not providing their children's developmental dependency needs.

5. By physically, emotionally, sexually, spiritually or verbally abusing them.

6. By using children to take care of their own unmet dependency needs.

7. By using children to take care of their marriages.

8. By hiding and denying their own shame based secrets (about addictions) to the outside world, so that children have to protect these covert issues in order to keep the family balance.

9. By not giving their time, attention and direction to their children so their children can develop a strong inner sense of self."

The ever increasing numbers of Alcoholics, Druga-holics, Workaholics, Sexaholics, Foodaholics and the increase in addictions to Power, Money, Possessions, and the inability to establish permanent relationships, have their roots in these old family practices.

Bradshaw's assessment is: "The crisis is far worse than anyone knows, because the adults who parent our children felt they were abandoned, and they are still separated from their own true inner selves. These parents are covering up their shame based inner selves. So the crisis is not just about how we raise our children, it's about a hundred million people who look like adults, talk and dress like adults, but are actually adult children.

These adult children run our families, our schools, our churches and our government. The real crisis is about adult children raising children who will also become adult children. It passes from one generation to the next."

Everyone who has learned to drive a car has had to take a driving course, but there is no required course for being a parent.

The purpose of the *Survival Handbook for Preschool Parents* is to explain the new and better ways to parent young children so they will learn to value themselves and know who they really are.

Learning the new parenting philosophy and skills can help parents understand the basic dependency needs of young children so they can replace the old shame based methods with real compassion and love. Today's children could then develop a strong sense of inner self, and love themselves as unique individuals with their own special potential who can then become mature adults with high Self-Esteem and a strong inner self.

Surviving as a Woman

How do you resolve the conflict you feel to be the woman you strive to be and the mother you need to be?

Women's Lib has caused a lot of confusion in the minds of mothers of young children.

The years of effort to attain a bachelor's degree, a master's degree, or a Ph.D.; the prestige of a rewarding career, the stimulation of interesting people—all fade into dim fantasy as you cope with the mundane "diaper and dishes" routine at home.

You really wanted this baby, but no one told you that you would be climbing the walls, trapped by a two-year-old tyrant.

After teaching several hundred mothers of all ages, economic levels, and educational levels, I have found that when a mother—single, married, younger or older—really understands how important she is to the healthy development of her child, she is happy to put off her career aspirations for the early years. She then sees mothering as a vital, challenging vocation and enjoys her child.

Father's Survival Kit

A mother and father who love each other should be the birthright of every child. A climate of love is a climate for healthy growth.

A father's sharing the responsibility of raising his children is now an accepted and encouraged innovation. With the increasing number of single parents, many fathers carry full responsibility for the children. If they marry again, they may acquire second families.

The new knowledge that a child's trust in himself and in you is determined in his first year (see pages 32–43) makes father's job very important on the day his child is born. How can a father convey love and acceptance to an infant? to a toddler? to a five-year-old?

You need to accept your feelings about the competition you now have for your wife's full time and attention. Sharing in the baby care and home chores can free her to spend more time with you. Loving support in the kitchen sparks romance in the bedroom.

What can a father do for an infant?

• Holding your baby gives him a sense of your warmth and strength. Your voice and responses are different, and experiencing them expands his experience of trust.

• Whether a baby is breast or bottle fed, father can take a turn holding baby and bottle when it's needed (especially at dinner time, when mother needs a boost and baby needs attention).

• Changing diapers may be difficult for some men, but it can be learned with practice. It is a proven fact that emotional attachment grows (both ways) when we assume the care of a helpless creature like a kitten, a puppy, and especially a baby.

• Baby has only one way to express his needs. Fussing and crying are signals that he needs something. You cannot spoil an infant with too much attention. The more he is cuddled and talked to, the better he will thrive and grow.

• Baby loves his bath, and father ought to share the excitement of the splashing water, floating toys, physical contact, and spontaneous fun.

• Father can add so much to the intellectual development of his child by playing the name game. Language is the basis of developing intelligence, so name what you feed him, what he is doing, where he is, and who he sees. The more a child sees and hears, the more he wants to see and hear. You can share the thrill of each new learning.

• If you have become friends with your baby the first year, you will be better able to handle the next stage of development, which is the most difficult for both mothers and fathers.

• The Toddler-Two may be more difficult for a father if his own experience as a child was to obey the master sergeant. You may unthinkingly handle your child in an autocratic manner unless you understand his needs. Learning unquestioned obedience is not a

Toddler's task and can stifle his autonomy and self-concept.
• Read and reread the section on autonomy (pages 44–51). Good parenting has to be learned and practiced just like any other skill.
• Take your child to work with you once in a while so he can understand what you do while you are away from him every day.
• Take your son to the hardware store and service station when you go. Let him watch you do your handyman jobs. He models after you and develops male goals and image.
• Your daughter needs your attention and your approval. When a girl is admired by her father, who tells her she is beautiful (regardless of her looks), she will feel beautiful all her life and enjoy being a girl.
• When you nurture your child, you give him the only thing no one else can give him—you give yourself.
• Enjoy him. That tells him you love him and builds his self-esteem. Then he can love you, too, as he grows up.

ADDITIONAL READING

Dodson, Fitzhugh, *How to Father,* pp. 1–67.
Gordon, Thomas, *Parent Effectiveness Training,* pp. 13–28.

Parents Make the Difference

The parent role is only a fraction of your life, but you, as a parent, are nearly 100 percent of the life of your dependent little person until he is three years old. Since Dr. Benjamin Bloom of the University of Chicago published his research, which showed that children attain 50 percent of their total mental ability by their fourth birthdays, the flood of proof that early learning is the key to life has made it mandatory that we help parents fulfill the vital role of teacher at home.

How does a parent help the child grow in these early years?

What kind of parenting produces the successful, happy, and creative child?

The "Hands off—he'll do it when he's ready" concept has been replaced by proof that the child learns faster and develops better when he has stimulating interaction with a loving mother and father. The more the child experiences in his world by seeing, doing, and talking about things, the more he learns and is capable of learning.

The day of fixed IQ is passed. With normal physical ability at birth, the mental potential of a child is limited only by the way his needs are met and the kind of loving stimulation he receives. This determines how he feels about himself.

The research of Dr. Jean Piaget in the development of intelligence proves that children need someone to respond to in order to grow intellectually and that learning comes with doing.

Columbia University used graduate students to play with and stimulate two-year-olds, trying to find out how much difference individual attention makes in the growth of intelligence. Fifty graduate students took fifty deprived children and spent one hour a day with each of them. They played games, took bus rides, went to the supermarket and zoo, and talked about what they had seen. After eight months these children were tested again, and the results showed that they had gained from two to ten points on an IQ test. The control group of the same number of children who did not have the individual attention stayed the same or lost a point or two. Only five hours a week of individual attention at this early age really counts!

There is an ever increasing wealth of research that shows the importance of mother-child interaction in the molding of healthy, well-adjusted children who are self-sufficient and creative and do well in school. Dr. Ira Gordon at the University of Florida has completed a four-year study on the effect of teaching, responsive mothers on children from the age of three months to four years. His program used parent educators who went into the homes and showed mothers how to talk to, stimulate, and respond to their infants from three months on. Children who had this stimulation were rated for their physical and intellectual development, initiative, and responsiveness. All children in the study rated higher than the control group at four years old. Children who started the mother interaction after their first birthdays did not rate as high as those who started at three months. The conclusion of this study is that the first year is critical in the child's development and that responsive mothers foster good development in the children.

Dr. Burton L. White of the Harvard Laboratory of Human Development, in seventeen years of research on children from birth to six, has concluded that a child's foundation for learning and living is set by his third birthday. He has found that it is almost impossible for parents and schools to undo the deprivation of the first three years.

Dr. White classified seventeen abilities that made children successful in school and also in life. Some of these abilities were

Getting and holding the attention of adults in socially acceptable ways (rather than with misbehavior)

Showing pride in personal accomplishment

Using resources effectively

Planning and carrying out complicated activities

Dealing in abstract thinking

Developing good language

Perceiving discrepancies, small details

Engaging in make-believe.

Leading and following peers

He rated children in three groups:

Group A Children who cope in a superior way in both social and academic situations.

Group B Children who are not incompetent, but who are not outstanding in any way.

Group C Children who are least able to interact with adults and who show negative social behavior and are lowest in intellectual competence.

He then set out to find how children developed these abilities. He started with the older children to try to find out what it was in each child's experience that made him an A, B, or C child. After working with six-year-olds, then five-year-olds, then four-year-olds, he found that what had happened between the child and the adults in his life before he was three determined his ability to meet the world in a successful manner.

MOTHERS OF GROUP A CHILDREN (10 percent of the total) did these things:

Child-proofed the home so the child could have the freedom to explore and discover.

Enriched the environment with toys and experiences.

Stopped to help the child with a problem and took time to explain what was happening.

Talked about everything they did.

Acted as a teaching resource, so the child felt free to consult and call for help.

Shared the child's excitement with each new accomplishment.

MOTHERS OF GROUP B CHILDREN (60 percent of the total) had this:

> A "live and let live" relationship. They were not designers of learning by giving undivided attention or enriching the environment.

MOTHERS OF GROUP C CHILDREN (30 percent of the total) were doing these things:

> Overprotecting their possessions (don't touch anything). This gives the child little freedom to explore and discover.

> Overprotecting the child. This limits his risks for fear of injury. Instead the mother should stand by to teach him how to go down a step, for example.

> Failing to communicate. This results in the child getting most of his language and experience from TV, so he doesn't develop good language skills.

> Not taking time to set up play situations.

> Showing no enjoyment in having the child around.

> Motivating the child by reward and punishment.

Parents can learn to do a superior job of rearing a child when they understand that they hold the key to his living and learning in his first three years.

All of us, mothers especially, ought to recognize very clearly that nurturing a baby is producing. Mothering is a way of producing a strong, healthy personality in a child. Our greatest national shortage is of completely sane people who feel secure inside themselves and who are glad they are who they are. There is no more significant job than that of producing healthy, happy human beings.

—*James L. Hymes, Jr.*

ADDITIONAL READING

Dodson, Fitzhugh, *How to Parent*, pp. 21–29, 280–284.

Hymes, James L., Jr., *The Child Under Six*, pp. 1–17.

White, Burton L., *The First Three Years of Life*, pp. 1–14.

Additional readings listed at the end of some chapters provide a planned study guide for teachers, parents, and groups.

Working Toward Maturity for Survival

The longer I work with people and examine my own experience, the more I observe that evolving maturity is life's process by which we grow both as parents and in all our relationships. Parenting is the opportunity to participate in life's process of maturation for ourselves and for our children.

I feel mature with high self-esteem when I *trust myself, honor my agreements, make commitments and keep them, am responsible,* and *trust others.* No one achieves all of these all the time or even at any one time. But the more I work to achieve them, the closer I am to a sense of mastery in my life.

Trusting myself comes and goes. I feel secure in some situations and with some people sometimes, and insecure at other times. When I am willing to accept *myself* as the cause of what happens in my life and become responsible for it, I trust myself.

I make agreements with others many times a day. I agree to be a loving mate, a good parent, a loyal friend, a productive employee. When I keep my agreements, my life works well and brings real satisfaction. I can trust myself and feel good about myself.

Commitment comes when I choose a realistic goal

and then work to attain what I have chosen. Very often I need to choose "the way it is" and become committed to it. Life works better when I "choose what I've got" and roll with the punches. I then trust myself rather than blame something or someone else.

Being responsible makes the difference between sacrifice (feeling put upon) and commitment (creating the result). I do not blame my parents, my circumstances, my mate, my children, or my boss for whatever problems I have. Responsibility begins with my willingness to accept *myself* as the cause of my problems.

When I don't trust myself, my self-esteem hits bottom, and I am miserable. When this happens, this process can help solve my problems:

STEP 1   Figure out where I am.

I am fifteen pounds overweight and always tired.

STEP 2   Figure out where I want to be.

I want to lose some weight and have more energy.

STEP 3   Decide what lies between me and my goal.

I look at my self-esteem, my feelings, my excuses.

STEP 4   Realize that the only thing between me and having what I want is *me*.

I can create the result I want or go on living with my excuses.

STEP 5   Set an attainable goal.

I could lose two pounds a week if I changed my diet sensibly and walked a mile a day.

STEP 6   Take responsibility for reaching my goal.

I am the center of who I am, what I do, and what I have. I will begin today, the only day that counts.

STEP 7   Forgive myself when I slip back, realizing that only I can attain my goal.

Each small success reinforces my commitment to reach my goal, and I begin to solve my problem.

When I use this process with anything that is a problem for me, I take responsibility and create a life that works. I trust myself and feel mature.

Trusting others (including my children) helps me allow them to be who they are. I will make the effort to be aware of their needs and feelings. I will accept what I like about my mate, my children, my parents, and my friends. I will also accept what I don't like about them. Trusting others is accepting them *just as they are.* Love comes with trust.

If I can stay senior (be adult) with my children in their early years, I can allow them some control over their own lives by empowering them to make some of their own choices. I will make agreements with them on daily tasks rather than try to control them with my power. I am then a partner, not a master.

When children learn to make choices, set goals, make and keep agreements, and take responsibility for what they do and who they are, they develop high self-esteem and act mature at an early age because they are self-disciplined.

What I do teaches more than what I say!

ADDITIONAL READING

Pritikin, Nathan, *The Pritikin Program for Diet and Exercise.* New York: Bantam Books, 1981.

Discipline and Survival

We need to be careful not to confuse discipline with punishment. The root word of *discipline* is *disciple*, which means "a follower." Our discipline should lead our children so they will accept our guidance and our values until they are mature enough to make their own decisions. Your need for power and your attitude toward each child determines what kind of discipline you will use.

The very nature of parenthood gives adults power over children. We're bigger, stronger, more experienced, and more verbal than they are. Since we live in a democratic society, we need to help our children function in a democratic way with self-control. There are three methods of dealing with children:

AUTOCRATIC   —I know what is best for you, and you must do it my way.

PERMISSIVE   —I allow you to do anything you want with no limits.

AUTHORITATIVE—I work with you for a solution that is acceptable to both of us.

Each of these methods produces a different personality in children. The way we feel about ourselves and our need to use power determine which method we use. Most of us will use the method on our children that was used on us when we were children. If our parents were democratic with us, we can allow our children to think for themselves. If our parents ruled with an iron hand, we instinctively use power, until we become enlightened and decide there is a better way.

THE AUTOCRATIC METHOD

An autocratic parent sees his child as a lump of clay to be molded as she sees fit. She needs to control him and make him do what she, the parent, wants. This puts the parent in the role of a dictator who not only makes the laws, but also has to enforce them. In order to enforce your rule, you will nag, reward, punish, scold, withdraw love, withhold food, spank, isolate, and take away privileges.

Autocratic discipline works while the child is young because he needs you so desperately that he will do anything you want, even while he resents you. A child is kept dependent with this kind of treatment. Any spark of independence is viewed as defiance of your authority. When the child is older, say ten or twelve, he doesn't need you so much because now he has friends who give him support. About this time you run out of power and cannot find a big-enough stick to enforce your rules. This kind of discipline breeds deep resentment, even hate, so the child will do whatever he needs to do to get out from under the stick.

What kind of people does this method develop? They will have low self-esteem because they have not been allowed to use any of their own ideas and talents. They are apt to lie because by telling the truth, they brought punishment down on their heads; no one took time to listen to their side of the story. They don't use their own initiative because someone else has made all the decisions for them. Their creative ability is nil because they were never given a chance to use it. These children are the trouble-makers in any group because they are constantly trying to prove their worth. These are the children who will do anything from stealing to smoking pot, if doing that will make them members of the gang. Since these children have had so little consideration at home, they seek it from their peer groups (kids their own age) and turn off their parents.

THE PERMISSIVE METHOD

The permissive discipline swept this country when parents were told that to set limits on a child would frustrate him, so many children were allowed more freedom than they could handle.

The real danger in this method is that the parent who is overpermissive cannot tolerate the behavior it brings out in the child. It makes the child selfish, inconsiderate, and with very low self-esteem that makes him the "brat" that his peers, his teachers, and his parents dislike. Being disliked by everyone keeps his opinion of himself at rock bottom. Being so miserable himself, he tries to make everyone else miserable.

Another damaging aspect of this relationship is the mixed messages the child receives from the unhappy parent. When a parent allows a child to behave in a way that is very annoying to her and doesn't do anything about checking the behavior, the child gets feelings of contempt, which he interprets as not being loved. He sees his parents as weaklings, and he feels lost and deserted. He, too, has to seek out his peers and do what they ask in order to survive.

THE AUTHORITATIVE METHOD

This is the most democratic method. Here parent and child share power, so both have their needs met This parent views her child as a separate person with intelligence and ability and a potential of his own that needs to be developed by allowing him to help make decisions and judgments about his own life.

With the authoritative method we are the strong adults that a child needs to bolster his own weakness and inexperience. We try to maintain a "sense of childhood" because we remember what we did as children and growing up takes about twenty years. Much of the behavior we would like to change is "just kids." Much of the learning they acquire about what is right, they learn by doing the wrong thing first. My byword was, "Hopefully, next time you can do better." Children need to know we expect the best from them. If we expect the worst, that's what they'll deliver.

We want to help our children learn to control their own behavior, so we begin at about two years to help children build a conscience. This we do by giving them some say-so in everyday events. For instance, your two-year-old comes to you just before dinner saying he is hungry and could he have a cookie. You know it will spoil his dinner, so you tell him no, and he is very unhappy. The same thing happens the second day, and you still say no. About the third day he will wait until you are out of the kitchen and get a cookie for himself. This is the beginning of devious and sneaky behavior.

If, when he asks for a cookie, you could say, "It's so near dinnertime, and I do want you to enjoy this good dinner I'm cooking. Would you like a half a cookie?" he will accept the half gladly, and he won't have to go behind your back. The same with the child who wants to go across the street to play with a neighbor child. He asks; you say no. He asks again and you say no, so he will go when you are not watching. Say yes as often as you can; then he will consult you. Children aren't always convenient, but if we follow through at this early age, they learn to control themselves and are much easier for the rest of their lives. If you both have needs, split them. There is a special program on TV, but it is bedtime. Compromise to resolve the conflict.

SPANKING

What about spanking? There are all degrees of spanking. Spanking as a way of controlling children may make them do what you want at the moment, but it breeds deep resentment and will not build self-control. There are emergencies when the danger to the child, like running in front of a car, is so great that you need drastic action to impress him. Spanking teaches a child to solve his problems with force and violence.

There is a time in the Two and Three stages when we need an enforcer because children are so willful and are such dawdlers. My method was, after all else had failed, to give a swat on the seat for emphasis. If you use it too often, you have to give bigger and bigger swats, and you are into spanking for control. There are many times when children need action rather than words. All children need to learn to respect authority without fear of punishment. There is a lot of difference between a quick swat and the threat of "If you don't do this, I will spank you."

Real democracy produces real people. Democracy in the home has far-reaching, positive benefits for our children. It nurtures the qualities we want in our children so we can enjoy them:

Self-respect	Nonaggressive leadership
Emotional stability	Meaningful involvement with
Self-confidence	life
Social responsibility	Development of potential
Friendly parent-child relationships	

There is no discipline but self-discipline.

ADDITIONAL READING

Briggs, Dorothy C., *Your Child's Self Esteem,* pp. 231–260.

Dodson, Fitzhugh, *How to Parent,* pp. 203–238.

Gordon, Thomas, *Parent Effectiveness Training,* pp. 1–28, 148–215.

Dinkmeyer, Don, and McKay, Gary D., *Parent's Handbook, Systematic Training for Effective Parenting,* A practical guide for the three- to twelve-year old.

Surviving Pregnancy

*The best chance a child has for a healthy
start in life is to be born to a healthy mother.*

So you are going to have a baby!

I hope you are excited about it and ready for it.

If you are one of the many who are not excited
and not ready for the news your body gives you, you
will soon discover there is no such thing as being
"sort of" pregnant. From this moment on, you will
never again have only yourself to consider. Your life
will never again be completely your own. But
motherhood can be beautiful.

Whether this baby was ordered or comes as a
surprise package, the miracle of life that has begun
needs all the help it can get from you.

PRENATAL CARE

As you reach for another soda cracker to quiet
your volcanic stomach, take every precaution to provide your developing child with the best possible
prenatal care.

Don't take any chances with the health of your
unborn child. See your doctor immediately and
follow his advice.

Both parents should seek out a class in prenatal care.

Most birth defects are caused in the first twelve weeks of pregnancy, when a baby's body, arms, legs, and internal organs are being formed.

Beware of viral infections. Thousands of children are deaf because their mothers had rubella (German measles) in their first three months of pregnancy.

Know your ancestors. Every couple should know their blood types so if there is a blood type conflict, precautions can be taken to prevent defects in the fetus.

Find out if there are any inherited defects or diseases in either family. If so, tell your doctor immediately. A new procedure called amniocentesis, which takes a sample of the fetal fluid, can predict whether the fetus is normal or defective. This knowledge can be very helpful to parents.

DRUGS AND SMOKING

Don't take any drugs without your doctor's prescription. Aspirin, antibiotics, laxatives, sleeping pills, tranquilizers, and narcotics can cause birth defects.

Alcohol passes through the placenta to the baby immediately. Too much alcohol can cause "fetal alcohol syndrome" and serious problems.

Don't smoke. Many doctors believe nicotine is directly responsible for stunting fetal growth since nicotine constricts the blood vessels. Smoking often replaces eating and deprives the fetus of adequate nutrition. Statistics show that smoking mothers have smaller babies. Infants weighing five and a half pounds or less at birth are more prone to health problems than those weighing seven pounds or more.

NUTRITION

Plan for good nutrition. The old program of eating for two (which produced plump babies and fat mothers) has been replaced by a balanced, high protein diet like the one on pages 59 to 61. Doctors no longer put pregnant women on scanty diets to keep them slim because these diets produced underweight babies who had many more health problems in the first year.

Malnutrition during pregnancy is a major cause of low birthweight, mental retardation, and later learning disabilities in the child. A mother's weight gain of at least twenty-four pounds with proper nutrition helps to ensure a healthy infant.

Keep a happy mental attitude. Serene mothers usually produce serene easy-to-live-with babies. There is no greater joy than having a happy, healthy baby.

Surviving the First Year

In the first year, a child needs to learn "I am."

The miracle of a healthy new baby is a unique thrill. A mother and father have every right to see it as a great accomplishment. Here is a completely helpless human being who will be dependent on you from now until he grows to independency.

He can sneeze, cough, suck, blink, yawn, and cry. He cannot lift his head, turn over, feed himself or see very well.

As his needs are satisfied by a loving, caring father and mother, he begins to feel that this world is a good place to be.

The human newborn is very demanding. He cannot wait for what he needs. When he is hungry, he needs to be fed immediately. When he is uncomfortable, he needs quick relief. Try to remember the last time you felt completely helpless and dependent on someone else to do everything for you. A baby feels this way all the time until he is past two and isn't really self-sufficient until his eighth birthday. He gradually learns independence but always falls back on you to reassure him.

LEARNING BASIC TRUST

Erik Erikson, the anchor of present thought on human development, tells us that the greatest need of a child in his first year is to learn basic trust. He learns to trust or distrust you, himself, and the world by the way he is treated. A child grows best in the loving reflections of a mother who enthusiastically reacts to each new step of growth. He becomes a person by responding to you, depending on you, and trusting that you will be there when he needs you and that you will gladly do what he needs.

The mother-child attachment is crucial following birth. A loving mother holds, talks to, and smiles at her infant, which is the stimulus he needs to grow physically, mentally, and emotionally. If a child does not form a strong interacting attachment with one mothering figure during his first year, his capacity to form loving relationships with other human beings seems to be permanently impaired. Studies of infants in institutions show that babies whose physical needs were met but who were deprived of voices and faces to respond to, things to look at and touch, and opportunities to observe and explore their world fail to develop physically and mentally and can actually be retarded in varying degrees.

A mother who responds to the needs and demands of a baby's body and mind teaches him once and for all that he can trust her, trust himself, and trust the world as a good place to be. Children who have not had these needs met fill the treatment centers for emotionally disturbed children.

There was Ralph, a four-year-old, in our nursery

school. He was handsome, healthy, and well dressed, but he could not relate to the other children or the teachers. He could not sit still and listen to a story and would not follow directions for the most ordinary tasks; he was devious in unacceptable activities and couldn't be trusted. Here was a boy from a wealthy family who had been given everything by his apparently concerned parents. The mystery of his behavior problems was finally revealed when we found out that he had been adopted as an infant at the insistence of the husband, while the wife didn't really want him. She took good care of his physical needs, bought lots of toys and clothes, but her underlying attitude was one of complete rejection. A child can be born perfectly normal, yet his intellectual and emotional growth can be retarded by indifference and negative attitudes.

A loving and accepting attitude toward a baby is much more important to his healthy development than the skill of keeping him clean and fed. The basic needs of a baby are food, warmth, and companionship. He is not capable of crying for anything he doesn't really need. When a baby has been fed and is dry and warm and still cries, he wants your company—and that's legal. Pick him up, cuddle him, talk to him, rock him for a while; reassure him that you are there when he needs you. But I can hear you say, "When do I get my work done?"

Your most important work in these early months is to nurture this little person—gladly. This is the age of complete dependency. When a baby can be completely dependent (you are there, gladly, when he needs you), he will move from dependency to more

independence, where he doesn't need you as often
or as much. If you let him cry it out, that is, force
him into independence too soon, he will hang on to
dependency and be very demanding of your attention indefinitely. When the need for dependency is
satisfied, it will disappear. So you have to walk the
floor a few nights. But when you understand this is
a legitimate need and the basis for a healthy personality, you will do it, gladly.

Let me caution you that a baby cannot sleep all
night and all day too. Be systematic about seeing
that he has some attention and diversion during the
day so he will be tired enough to sleep at night.

You don't teach a baby who is boss by letting him
cry too long. What he is learning is that the world
is a cold, cruel place, and nobody cares about his
need for comfort. When he feels sure of you—basic
trust—then he can begin to depend on himself and
not need you as often or as long at a time. He will
be more content when he is awake and will amuse
himself for short intervals.

Relaxed mothers help their babies feel secure.
Infants are quick to sense tension, either with themselves or other family members. Calm mothers usually
have happy babies. The best environment for healthy
growth is created by a calm, caring, compassionate
mother.

SLEEPING HABITS

How do we help a baby develop good sleeping
habits?

As soon as he comes home from the hospital,
establish a sleep routine and for the first four to six

months follow it every time you put him to bed.

After he has been fed and changed, put him in his bed gently; talk softly as you rub his back or head to help him relax. Give him a pacifier and a kiss on the cheek and say goodnight. Leave the room and close the door partway so you can hear him.

What's happening when he cries bitterly and doesn't go to sleep? He may be fearful and need more assurance or maybe he just can't relax. The harder he cries, the more upset he becomes.

Go to him again and, without picking him up, go through the sleep routine again. You may need to stay ten minutes, rubbing his back and softly singing or talking to him. A musical Teddy Bear or music box is a relaxing sound. Turn it on, say goodnight, and leave the room.

If he has worked himself into a frantic tizzy, wrap him tightly in a light blanket, arms inside, and hold him close to you with his head next to your heart while you rock him and talk or sing softly until he is calm and relaxed. This usually works on a child until he is two or more.

There may be times when you'll need to use the sleep routine up to five times, but he learns what to expect—he is learning to trust you and will go to bed happily and drop off to sleep.

If you have tried all these tricks and he still screams, call your pediatrician.

There comes a time when babies are about four months old (sometimes older) when they seem to be testing. You have done everything to make your baby comfortable when you put him down to sleep.

When you leave the room, he starts to cry. You return and pick him up, and he's ready to play games. You put him down, and he cries even harder.

You will soon sense when he is "working you for attention." At this point you need to take a stand and hold firm. When he cries, wait a few minutes, then go to him, gently put him down again, kiss him goodnight, and walk out. Be pleasant, but firm.

After a third time of this routine, close the door as you say goodnight and let him cry it out. He will fall asleep eventually. When he learns that a loving goodnight means sleep time, bedtime can be beautiful. Don't weaken or he will run the show indefinitely.

FEEDING METHODS

What about the breast versus bottle controversy? I am convinced that any mother who really wants to nurse her baby can be successful. The intimacy, dependency, warmth, and healthful convenience of breast feeding enhances a close bond between mother and child and helps to build basic trust.

A mother in one of my classes had an adopted son and followed the usual procedure of formula feeding. When she adopted an infant daughter five years later, she was determined to nurse her. She studied and followed *The Womanly Art of Breast Feeding* by the La Leche League International. In two weeks her milk came in, and she was nursing this baby adequately for the next six months. She felt her daughter was much more secure, trusting, and spontaneously outgoing because she had been breast fed.

If you choose bottle feeding, be sure to hold your baby and his bottle. He can feel close and confident

when you make this a very special time for the two
of you.

If you want to nurse twins, but only have enough
milk for one baby, I suggest nursing one baby all
day one day while the other baby has formula all
day. Alternate so each baby is breast fed every other
day. I found alternating breast and bottle every
other feeding a dismal failure. The staying power of
the two kinds of milk is so different that neither
baby was satisfied.

DEMANDS

Babies are very demanding, messy, fussy, noisy,
inconvenient, and time consuming. Their only thanks
to us is a sweet smile, a cute gurgle, a wild flapping
of hands and feet, and, later on, a big hug. We get
weary. We'd like an uninterrupted meal, a full
night's sleep, a clean house, and time for a book.

Perpetual sweetness and light are not required for
an emotionally stable baby.

If your patience with a screaming baby gives out
in a brewing clash of your needs versus his needs,
what can you do? Hand him over to his father or
another adult to calm him while you pull yourself
together. His fear feeds on your anxiety. If you are
alone, change your focus from your fear to doing
something to calm him. The snug blanket trick will
usually work here.

No harsh words or loud voices for babies.

No physical punishment for babies.

Accept yourself as human. Each time you calm
him will make the next crisis easier to handle. This,
too, shall pass as he grows and as you learn his
special needs.

Cherish your baby. Smile at him. Sweet-talk him. Whisper in his ear that you're glad you have him. Babies can't be spoiled with love and attention.

If he doesn't fit your schedule, check your priorities.

When he cries, stop for a few minutes and give him your undivided attention. Change his position, provide a new interest. Put him on a blanket on the floor with things to look at and handle. A quick five minutes will satisfy him, and you can have an hour to get your work done. When we put our children first, housework doesn't worry us as much.

When he cries as you leave him or is afraid of strangers (about six months), pat yourself on the back for having established a good attachment with him. He now knows who he belongs to, and that's very important in his healthy development.

DEVELOPMENT

An infant's intelligence begins to develop the day he is born. His brain registers stimulation from his ears, eyes, and skin.

You can encourage development by making lots of sounds with your voice, by playing music, by clapping your hands, or by snapping your fingers. Change the direction of the sound to see if he follows it.

Babies respond to color and pattern. There was an experiment in which three masks—one plain, one striped, and one shaded to resemble a human face— were shown to three-week-old infants. They didn't respond to the plain or striped one but registered excitement when they saw the facelike mask. These infants were already responding to their environment, especially when it resembled their mother.

A baby learns from skin contact. Gentle handling; rubbing his back, legs, and arms; putting on warm, dry clothes; and holding him snug and close gives him the contact stimulation he needs in the first three months of life.

From three to six months, he uses his hands in active exploration. He practices reaching for objects he can see. He needs ordinary, safe household items like cups, bowls, pans, plastic bottles, and scraps of bright cloth he can manipulate and experiment with. He can now make things happen in his environment.

From now until he is twelve or fifteen months old, he will sit up, creep, pull himself up, and eventually walk, exploring every nook and cranny of the house.

Repetition is the name of his game. He does everything again and again until he perfects the skill.

What about playpens?

You may feel like the mother who sat in one an hour a day to get some rest.

Actually a playpen serves two good causes: you know where your baby is, and he learns to play alone. Be sure to place it where he can see you.

Beginning at about three months, a baby can be put in his playpen an hour twice a day. When he has some toys, he begins to entertain himself. Every mother has times when the phone or washer takes her attention. A baby is safe in a playpen.

There is a real danger in using it too often. Babies four to eight months old need to learn to creep because creeping plays a very important part in mental development and learning physical coordination.

A playpen is a lifesaver in the toddler stage. If you have been consistent with using it an hour a couple of times a day, the toddler will accept it as his playtime place.

The secret of childhood is the inner power to grow and develop as a unique individual. The secret of good parenting is to guide the child and remove the obstacles in his way.

When a child can grow in the sunshine of unconditional love from the adults in his life, he can use his own power to develop physically, emotionally, and intellectually into a real person who likes himself and who likes others, including his parents.

When a mother gives of herself with love, she is investing her life, day by day, in her child, who will bring lasting dividends of joy. Without love and invested time, her dividends can be endless disappointments. I know of no area of life where we reap exactly what we sow as we do in raising our children.

ADDITIONAL READING

Briggs, Dorothy C., *Your Child's Self Esteem*, pp. 72–81.

Dodson, Fitzhugh, *How to Parent*, pp. 40–73.

Hymes, James L., Jr., *The Child Under Six*, pp. 18–41, 63–73.

White, Burton L., *The First Three Years of Life*, pp. 15–102.

Survival Hints for the First Year

Pick your baby up and talk to him when he isn't crying; otherwise you are conditioning him to have to cry to get your attention.

When he is a month old, prop him up in his infant seat near where you are so he can see the world around him and watch you working and moving around. He'll sleep better if he has been close to you and has had some stimulation several times a day.

If you nurse your baby, enjoy it so he will feel that he is precious and dear to you. Your feelings let him know that this is the most important thing you have to do. He will also get your feelings if you try to make him "hurry up" so you can get on with more important things.

If you use bottle feeding, take time to hold him and the bottle—gladly. Talk to him and enjoy him. This undivided attention reassures him, so he can separate from you more easily when it's time to go to bed.

Remember that children have a radar sense that records your feelings. When he cries at night, try to be gracious as you satisfy his needs. Sweet talk and angry feelings are very confusing to children. Unconditional love is the climate for healthy mental and emotional growth.

The special nature of a young child is helplessness. Having so little power within himself, his greatest needs are

Will they be here when I need them?

Will they be able to do what I need them to do?

Will they be glad to do it?

Babies are not spoiled by our love and attention. Loving and enjoying them is the sunshine that nourishes healthy growth.

Babies make their own comforters, which serve a basic purpose. When he has his bottle, thumb, pacifier, blanket, or favorite toy, he makes up for our shortcomings, humans that we are. So don't be in a hurry to take them away. He will give them up when he is more sure of himself and you.

The development of basic trust in a consistent mothering figure is the strong foundation for the building of healthy personality in each child. Lack of it forces a child to turn inward, which can be the groundwork for later mental illness.

Allowing him to be completely dependent by satisfying his needs during the first year prepares him for the steps toward increasing independence, confidence, and the desire to try new things for himself.

Surviving with a Toddler-Two

From the first to the third birthday,
the child needs to learn "I can."

One of the most critical stages of development takes place between eight and twenty-four months—the Toddler-Two stage. Most parents cope with and enjoy an infant, but many parents are threatened by the move toward autonomy of the Toddler-Two.

This is the autonomous stage, when he moves from dependency, with you making all the decisions for him, to increasing independence, when he struggles to have some control over himself and his world. At this age he will vacillate between dependence and independence. One minute he wants your help, and the next he won't let you touch him.

Babies are fairly easy to live with, but when your toddler says NO! NO! NO! to everything you suggest, he is not convenient or considerate, and his determination will challenge all the love and patience you can muster for the next two years.

As a Toddler-Two he needs to gain a sense of autonomy (self-control), which is so necessary for the development of a good self-image. When he begins to walk, accept him as a member of the family with special needs. Childproof your house. Put away fragile wedding presents for a couple of years and allow him the freedom to touch and explore anything he can reach. If you say no every time he tries to explore, you will destroy the creativity and curiosity, which is the learning how to learn, in the bud.

This is the age of "Me do." He is testing and training his own abilities, learning to make choices, and taking the risks he needs to prove to himself and to you that he is a separate person. His explorations teach him ideas of mass, weight, and cause and effect.

A child's attitude toward life and learning is formed by the reactions of his parents. When he pulls all the pans out of the cupboard and his mother smiles and says, "What have you found?" he will feel very different than if she scolds, "You're making a mess." This is the period when he learns that curiosity is good or bad. If it's bad, learning is thwarted.

When he can feel, touch, put together, and manipulate all kinds of materials around his home, he feels the sense of accomplishment that makes him feel BIG, which is the greatest need at this point in his life.

When he has achieved a new learning or skill, praise him with "What a BIG boy" because that is what he so desperately wants to be. When you say, "You're a good boy," it is a moral judgment he cannot comprehend.

If we are training a dog, we use "good boy" to get

obedience. With children, we want to teach them to strive with their own power.

If we help him feel BIG, he will try all the harder to be BIGGER.

Say, "I just can't believe you're big enough to put on your own clothes." He'll try very hard to show you that he is BIG enough.

If he is not allowed this freedom to experiment and discover, he will doubt his own ability and develop a low self-image.

He needs to feel *competent* (able to do things), which he does with each new learning. Then he will feel *confident* (capable) in his own ability to manage himself and his world.

Does he need any limits? Yes! If what he is trying to do affects his health, safety, or the property of others, you say no and stand firm. If you haven't used no for a lot of unimportant things, your no will have real meaning when there is an emergency. These emergencies need action. Don't yell no; go get him and carry him away from the danger.

Are there ways to move a Toddler-Two in the direction he needs to go and still not destroy his self-esteem?

Positive Commands. The first skill for handling young children is to learn to use positive commands. When we tell someone not to do something, they are more determined than ever to do it their way. Instead of saying "Don't touch," say "Put it back" or "Bring it to me." Instead of saying "Don't go in the street," say "Stay on the sidewalk." Rather than saying "Don't eat with your fingers," say "Please use your spoon." This is the most effective skill a mother can learn. Teachers know it works.

Claudia was bringing her two children to the YWCA for class. They were two-and-a-half years and ten months. When she tried to gather her belongings from the car, the two-and-a-half-year-old kept running away across the parking lot. Claudia decided to try a positive command. "Mommy needs your help when we get out of the car. Will you please put both your hands on the front fender so the car won't move?" The child was completely dedicated to her job. After her mother had baby, diaper bag, and belongings in hand, she said, "Thanks for helping," and took the little girl's hand, and they walked in together. A positive command works wonders.

It is a skill you can learn. After you've had a confrontation, think about how a positive command could have avoided the conflict. When you give a positive command, you are gradually relaxing your control, and the child is more willing to cooperate when he has some control over his actions. He doesn't have to fight you, so it avoids confrontations.

Distraction. Since a Toddler-Two has a very short attention span, we will capitalize on it to move him. Distraction is a very effective way to divert him from things you do not want him to do. He is into the fireplace ashes, so you say "Come help me move this chair" or "Let's go get your choochoo train." Children this age love to be helpful, so give them small jobs to divert them. If you provide acceptable activities, you won't have to use as many diversionary tactics.

Substitution. When a child is doing something unacceptable, offer him an acceptable alternative. If he brings you the butcher knife, offer him a safe utensil in exchange. When you shop in the supermarket, provide him with animal crackers to keep him occupied so he won't need to clean off all the shelves while you are busy shopping.

Allowing choices. This is a very effective way to get children to cooperate. When a child balks, give him a legitimate choice. "You may sit up to the table and eat your dinner, or you may get down. Which do you choose?" Not "If you don't eat your dinner, you have to leave the table." (That's a threat.) Say, "You need a wrap. Do you want your coat or your sweater?" Not "You can't go out without your coat." (That's a negative command.)

Anyone, including children, will do anything more willingly if they have some say-so in the matter. Giving choices allows the child to decide what he is going to do, so there is no need for strong-armed punishment to get things done. It helps develop self-control, judgment, initiative, and cooperation.

If he is strong-armed, he will be rebellious, aggressive or submissive, and a general nuisance. This is a master-slave relationship and breeds deep resentment and low self-image.

There are two phrases that are used in nursery schools and can be very helpful to mothers. The first is "*You need to.*" Not "I say you have to" or "If you don't, you'll get the wooden spoon" but simply, "You need to"—because that's the way it is in this world.

"You need to go to sleep" or "You need to sit on this chair."

"You may not" asserts direction without threat. "You may not hit the baby" or "You may not go out in the rain." No threat—just a clear-cut statement of ground rules for acceptable behavior. Children need clear-cut authority, without fear of rejection and punishment. This leads to self-direction, our ultimate goal.

A good sense of timing helps avert confrontations with young children. Be sure the child is hungry when you expect him to eat. See that he has had enough activity to be tired enough to sleep. Understand that Toddler-Twos are on the move and can't be expected to sit patiently in restaurants and doctors' offices or even at the family dinner table. He'll learn this much later.

Around two and a half, children have a sense of organization. They want the light on, a certain toy, a glass of water. Capitalize on this by establishing a regular routine for meals, play, naps, and bedtime. Children feel more secure when they can depend on a schedule. Bedtime can be beautiful with a quiet story and some undivided attention before the child has to stay alone.

Remember when he says NO, he is not being defiant. He is just practicing his "person homework." Even when he says no to a dish of ice cream, if we accept his no as a push for independence and don't force it, he will immediately want the ice cream. Let him have it, gladly, and know that he was just testing to see if you would allow him to make a decision for himself. Yes, starting at the tender age of two.

When a child reaches three, with a good sense of autonomy, he will be confident, capable of doing many things for himself, and easier to live with.

If he has been blocked too often and forced too much to comply with your demands, with no consideration for his ideas and feelings, he will have to prove that he *IS* somebody with unacceptable behavior. He carries over his hitting and possessive behavior into three and even longer because he hasn't been allowed to develop his autonomy. When he knows he can own it, he will be willing to share.

Nobody enjoys a child like this. Since no one likes him, he can't like himself. Hence there is low self-esteem and problem behavior.

If two children two and a half or older are hitting, pushing, and grabbing when they have to be together, it seems to help if you calmly lead the troublemaker to a small chair and tell him he needs to sit there a few minutes. The chair needs to be where you are. This may help break the cycle without destroying autonomy. Be aware that another child in your house is a threat to the domain of your own child at this age. Isolation is not the answer. Your child can't learn to live with other people while he's in a room by himself.

Separation can be a problem around the second birthday. There are a few precautions that can help.

• Always have a new baby-sitter come early or, for a while, the day ahead to get acquainted with your child. The child needs to transfer his trust from you to someone new, so he needs your help.

• If you leave him in a church nursery or play center and he screams, stay with him until he gets to know one of the workers by name and feels comfortable. I taught church nursery for ten years after staying with one of our daughters "for a little while" and enjoyed every minute of it. Volunteer to help until your child adjusts.

ADDITIONAL READING

Briggs, Dorothy C., *Your Child's Self Esteem*, pp. 124–131.

Dodson, Fitzhugh, *How to Parent*, pp. 74–120.

Hymes, James L., Jr., *The Child Under Six*, pp. 93–101, 117–157.

White, Burton L., *The First Three Years of Life*,
8–14 months: pp. 103–150
14–24 months: pp. 151–189
24–36 months: pp. 191–212.

Survival Hints for Toddler-Twos

Educational psychologists have proved in research that reinforcement is a powerful teaching tool. When a child, or anyone, receives attention or reward for an action (reinforcement), he will do it again.

We use this a hundred times a day with children, so we need to understand how to use reinforcement to encourage acceptable behavior. We are apt to make the mistake of reinforcing only the unacceptable behavior. When a child is playing quietly, causing no trouble, we don't say a word. The minute he steps out of line, we make big noises. He's learning that he can't get our attention when he's playing quietly, so he'll try something that will get our attention.

Ignore behavior you don't want (no reinforcement) unless it threatens his health or safety or the safety or property of others. If it does, take action. Acknowledge behavior you do want (reinforcement).

A universal problem with Toddler-Twos—children between eight and twenty-four months—is turning on the TV. The easiest way to handle it is to put it out of his reach for this year or remove the knobs. This, too, shall pass.

If you can't move it, realize that when he turns it on for the first time, he gets marvelous reinforcement. Sound, color, and action! Besides that, he gets a big rise out of you (reinforcement), so he tries it again and again. The more you react, the more he'll go back to it (repeated reinforcement), and it becomes a power struggle.

If, when he turns it on, you don't react, he has only the new experience of the TV to reinforce his action. Let him work it through until the newness wears off, and he'll lose interest in it and move on to something else. As with much of his learning, when his curiosity is satisfied, he'll try something new.

Make it a point to let him turn it on for his programs, like "Sesame Street," and also let him turn it off when it's over. He feels big when he has control.

Little boys are more apt to be very persistent. To save your own ears and the confrontation, find an old radio that the child can have. Tell him he can turn it on as often and as loud as he wants in his own room, but he *may not* turn on the TV because "Too much TV gives Mommy a headache."

Children who are provided with interesting things to do, indoors and outdoors, don't depend on TV as much for amusement.

Remember to praise him when he's doing what you want him to do. "It's so nice to see you are enjoying that game." This is reinforcement for acceptable behavior.

TANTRUMS

Tantrums and Twos go together. It helps if we understand what causes them so we can keep them to a minimum. A Toddler-Two is his own worst enemy. He is constantly trying to do things he does not have the size, the strength, or the coordination to do. He tries to put the square peg in the round hole, carry things that are too heavy for him, and reach things that are too high for him, and when he fails, he bursts out crying in complete frustration and anger. He is angry at himself, at you, and at the world. This is not the time to shame him. Anger is a good and necessary emotion, and we need to accept his feelings by saying, "I can see you are very unhappy." At this point walk away until he cools down. Then he needs a calm, close hug to reassure him and encourage him to try again. All of life is made up of "try agains."

We need to protect Twos as much as possible from too many really frustrating crises. Here is where you use your distraction and substitution to redirect the child's interest. Plan ahead to avoid as much trouble as you can. Remove the temptations if you can, and provide toys and equipment he can use and enjoy without too much frustration.

Tantrums are more apt to happen if children are overtired. Long shopping tours and long car rides ask for tantrums. Too many tantrums at this age should tell you that you are expecting too much of him and you need to scale down his environment to fit his needs. A little boost with a problem like helping him unhook his bike wheel from the table leg or helping with a block game he can't manage will relieve his frustration and assure him that you understand his problem. Use your positive skills and this, too, shall pass.

CHILDREN CLOSE TOGETHER

It is a mystery where the myth began that good spacing for children in a family is two years apart. I suspect that when mothers nursed their babies for two years and didn't get pregnant, it just happened that way and became accepted practice. When anyone asks me for my recommendation on spacing children, I shout loud and clear, four years apart! Many psychologists suggest a minimum of three years between children.

A child does not become a self-sufficient individual until his fourth birthday. By this time he can take care of most of his needs without the constant help and supervision he has needed until now. During the Toddler-Two stage a child's greatest need is his mother's constant interest and attention. Just keeping up with him is a twenty-four-hour job.

If a new baby intrudes, either by accident or design, and takes the mother's energy and attention, the Toddler-Two may be slighted just because it is physically impossible for one mother with only two hands to satisfy the needs of both children. Another hazard is the pressure and fatigue that makes it very hard for the mother to be patient.

While the Toddler-Two is trying to work through his dependency stage, his needs are the same as the new baby's needs. If a mother understands that a Toddler-Two doesn't graduate from this demanding stage when a new baby comes, she will make every effort to meet his needs as a Two and not expect him to suddenly be grown-up.

So many of the mothers with whom I deal do have two children under three, and when they understand that the Toddler-Two needs as much time and attention as if he were the only child, there are fewer problems. My observation has been that when a mother gives the Toddler-Two his just dues and doesn't expect more than two-year-old behavior, the older child accepts the baby and is not damaged by the intrusion.

Children close together who love each other while they are growing up had their individual needs met at the Toddler-Two stage. Each child needs some undivided attention from mother each day. A story, a game, a walk, or a trip to the store with just the two of you lets each child know he can depend on you for the strength he does not have.

DEALING WITH CHILDREN'S FEARS

Fear is a very real emotion. The problem with fear in children is that we don't know which is real and which is imagined fear. To the child, either one can be very frightening. We don't help a child by trying to talk him out of his fear. It is much better to accept it and try to understand it.

Often fear is a gimmick to keep your company a little longer. This is a signal that your child needs more of your attention during the day. If he is really afraid, stay with him until he feels better or falls asleep. We can only help him become strong by helping him overcome these small weaknesses. If he wants to crawl into your bed, patiently take him back to his own bed and stay with him until he falls asleep. This may take a few nights, but allowing him to stay with you is making him more dependent on you, and that is not healthy for either of you. A timer can be a help here. Have him help you set the timer and tell him you can stay until it dings. Some extra time and attention at these times satisfies a need and helps the problem disappear. A small night-light in his room may make him more comfortable.

There are three things you cannot do for anyone else (including your children)—eat, sleep, and go to the toilet;

or

You can lead a horse to water, but you can't make him drink!

EATING

Eating problems can begin with overanxious mothers. Remember, children will eat when they are hungry, so our job is to plan their meals and offer them an attractive, well-balanced diet and see that they get outdoor exercise so they will be hungry.

As you move from breast or bottle feeding to more solid food, don't get excited if the child doesn't like a new food the first time. Let it go by and try again later. If he doesn't like cereal but likes fruit, put cereal on the spoon first and tip it off with fruit, and he'll get both. Introduce a new flavor with a familiar one.

Allow him to dislike some foods without making

a big fuss. Keep coming back to them. If you don't make a big deal of it, he will learn to eat a variety of foods. Show him you enjoy feeding him; talk to him and keep it pleasant. Limit his quantity of milk as he eats more solid foods so he won't be too full.

At about four to six months, give him finger foods like Zwieback or Cheerios. This helps build the co-ordination he needs to feed himself. As he grows, try wiener circles, and cooked cut green beans and diced carrots. He will enjoy feeding himself and will soon want to use a spoon.

When a Two or Three stalls on food, just spoon it to him or ask him to take two bites of each thing on his plate. Variety of food is more important than quantity.

What about the "You can't have dessert unless" problem? If you have planned a nutritious meal, the dessert should be part of the balance, like milk pudding or fruit. Better to treat dessert as part of dinner. So you can say "When you've eaten two bites of this and this, I'll be glad to give you the rest of your dinner." There are many fat people in this country who were trained to put such great importance on desserts that it is now a problem to them.

Children have pretty much formed their eating patterns by their second birthday. If you haven't made a battle of it, they will continue to try new foods. If they don't eat much at one meal, they will probably make up for it the next. Their appetites vary so much, you need to look at the whole day to judge if the intake is adequate.

A guideline for a day is two foods out of each of the following groups sometime through the day.

Key Nutrients Needed Daily for an Adequate Diet

	Where Found	*Needed For*
PROTEINS	meat, poultry, fish, milk, cheese, eggs; dried peas and beans, seeds; nuts and peanut butter; whole-grain bread; whole-grain cereals; wheat germ, high protein cereals	building and repairing body tissues, bone, blood, hair, skin, and muscle; energy; building resistance to infection
CALCIUM	milk, milk dishes, cheese; leafy green vegetables; soy beans, brown rice; whole grains, nuts and sprouts	forming teeth and bones; blood coagulation; muscle growth and function
IRON	lean meat, liver, egg yolk; whole-grain cereals and breads, dried peas, beans, and potatoes; all fresh fruits and vegetables	functioning of red blood cells (There is an alarming increase in iron deficiency in young children.)
STARCHES	spaghetti, corn meal, macaroni; whole-wheat flour; whole-grain cereals	energy
FATS	cream, oils, butter, nuts, margarine, cheese	energy

	Where Found	*Needed For*
NATURAL SUGARS	fruits, raisins, dates, honey	energy
REFINED SUGAR	(White sugar contains empty calories and no nutrients.)	energy (Infantile diabetes can be triggered by too much soda pop, sugared cereals, candy, and sweets.)

The fuel we put into the machine determines the way it functions.

The easiest way to add good nutrition to your family's diet is to make or buy whole-wheat or whole-grain bread, rolls, and hamburger buns.

Enriched white flour has had more than a score of essential nutrients removed to prolong shelf life. These nutrients are fed to animals that are better nourished than our children are.

Whole-wheat flour retains the wheat germ plus the natural bran. This provides protein, B vitamins, Vitamin E, Vitamin A, minerals (including iron), unsaturated fatty acids, and fiber.

Cookies, muffins, pancakes, and carrot cake made with whole-wheat flour are nutritiously delicious.

If a child is bored and fussy, start an interesting activity instead of giving him a cookie. Learning to depend on food for entertainment and comfort can be a big fat problem later on.

SUGGESTIONS FOR A HEALTHFUL, BALANCED DAILY DIET

BREAKFAST	Orange juice (to be sure we get Vitamin C for healthy cells)
	Choice of oatmeal, high-protein dry cereal, egg, French toast, pancakes, muffins, or cottage cheese on toast
	Milk
LUNCH	Choice of cheese, peanut butter, tuna, or canned meat sandwiches; beef franks; cottage cheese
	Soups, tomato juice, V-8 juice
	Fresh vegetable strips (carrots, celery, zucchini, cherry tomatoes, avocado, olives, cut green beans dipped in mayonnaise)
	Canned or fresh fruit
	Milk or yogurt
DINNER	Meat, meat loaf, hamburger casseroles, tuna casseroles, poultry, fish, cheese, devilled eggs, baked beans, chili, sloppy joes
	1 yellow and 1 dark green vegetable
	Salad or relishes of fresh vegetables
	Milk puddings, apple slices, orange cartwheels, bananas, Jell-O with fruit
	Milk
SNACKS	Cheese cubes, hard-boiled eggs, oranges, apples, bananas, fruit leathers, oatmeal cookies, Triscuits, Wheat Chex, raisins, Cheerios

Two paperback books that are very helpful in understanding and planning good nutrition are

Feel Like a Million by Catharyn Elwood (Pocket Books).

Let's Cook It Right by Adelle Davis (New American Library) (my favorite easy-to-use complete cookbook).

There is only one general statement you can make about children and that is that no two of them are alike.

SLEEPING

Timing is the key to establishing good sleep habits. Be sure the child is tired when you expect him to sleep. Fresh air and exercise help. Sleep can be beautiful if you follow a regular routine. Naptime comes after lunch and a story. After dinner in the evening, there should be some undivided attention at any age, from holding an infant to a game with a five-year-old. Then, undress for bed, a story, a favorite toy to sleep with, a small night-light in his room, a special hug, and a goodnight kiss.

When you put him down, say, "Isn't this a good bed! Doesn't it feel comfy?"

If you are putting a child to bed to get him out of your hair, don't let him know it, or he will fight it indefinitely.

If you require a lot of sleep and your child doesn't,

it really is hard on you, but recognize your differences and reach the best solution you can. This, too, shall pass.

About the third birthday some children will balk at taking a nap. Even if all children don't need the sleep every day, they do need a change of pace. Tell him he doesn't have to go to sleep, just to rest quietly. "This is our quiet time." Keep a supply of the little inexpensive children's books you buy at the supermarket and let him choose one for you to read to him and three he can read in bed by himself. This has several advantages:

- When he relaxes looking at a book, he will usually drop off to sleep. If he doesn't sleep, make it clear that he stays in or on his bed till the clock has gone around once (one hour).

- It encourages his interest in books and quiet play, which are so necessary for reading readiness.

- It gives you relief from the constant supervision so you can rest or do something for yourself.

- I *know* young children are better company at dinnertime if they've had a rest. You'll cope better if you've had one too.

TOILET TRAINING

Our society puts great pressure on mothers to be successful at toilet training—so much so that many mothers are very anxious about it.

There are some guiding principles. Children vary

in their readiness, but most children are not physically developed enough to control the bladder and bowels until they are past two. If you put a child on the potty every two hours and are successful before he is two, you probably are the one who is trained.

His need for autonomy is so important here. If you set the stage and let him take some responsibility, he will cooperate—sooner or later. If it is taken out of his hands, he may use the whole business as a weapon against you.

There are some hints that can make it easier.

At about two or two and a half, talk about how big boys stay dry by using the toilet. Shop for some new "big boy" training pants and some new elastic top, easy-to-pull-down long pants. Let him help pick them out. Be sure they are large enough to pull down easily. Keeping a girl in dresses during the training period seems to help. Practice with him in pulling his pants down and up again while he is dressing. When you can stay home for three days, let him decide which day he will discard his diaper and put on the new pants.

Put his potty chair in the kitchen, where you will be most of the time. Half of the problem of going to the bathroom is the separation and isolation from you. Better to be where you are. Give him extra liquid so he needs to go often. Let him know he is on his own to go to the potty when he needs to. If two hours (or his normal interval) have gone by and he hasn't gone, have the timer ding and say, "The bell says it's potty time." Give him a choice. "Do you want my help, or can you go alone?" (Either choice gets him there.) After he pee-pees in the potty, show your excitement. "You did it!" "Big boy!" Positive reinforcement and increasing autonomy help this learning process.

Bringing a child through potty training with confidence in himself is so important that we cannot afford to be impatient and belittling. Play it cool and roll with the punches. The less pressure you assert, the quicker he'll cooperate. If he doesn't succeed the first time, put his diapers back on with as little fuss as possible and wait two or three months more. He may not be ready yet. Accept it gracefully. Watching an older child perform will spur him to want to use the toilet too. At first, try sitting him on the toilet facing the tank and wall. Both boys and girls like to see what they are accomplishing and in that position are not as fearful of falling into the water.

When he trains himself, he is very proud. More and more control of himself builds his self-esteem, which shows in his happy disposition and cooperative behavior.

CHANNELING NEEDS

At this age there seem to be inborn needs to be satisfied. If a child is climbing everything and everywhere, provide an acceptable substitute like a four-foot ladder or a climbing dome. He needs to work this through.

When he persists in an unacceptable activity (pouring his juice on the floor), think of some way he can get the experience in an acceptable manner (water play at the sink). As soon as it is satisfied, it usually disappears.

AT THE DOCTOR'S OFFICE

Plan ahead and make the long waits in doctors' offices an opportunity for some special undivided attention for your child. Take a couple of favorite books and a game that you can enjoy together.

Note: If you want to understand how your two-year-old feels about the new baby, imagine your husband, after two years of wedded bliss, saying, "I have a nice surprise for you! I'm bringing home a new wife so you'll have a playmate!"

Caution: Nursing a baby is *not* a dependable birth control method. Consult your doctor or the Planned Parenthood Association in your community for reliable options in family planning.

ADDITIONAL READING

Smith, Dr. Lendon. *Improving Your Child's Behavior Chemistry.* New York: Pocket Books, 1978 (paperback).

——. *Feed Your Kids Right.* New York: McGraw-Hill, 1979 (paperback).

Don'ts and Dos for Toddler-Twos

Don't expect a Toddler-Two to come when you call across the supermarket or if he is running toward the street. He is not yet intellectually ready to follow rules or verbal directions at a distance.

Do go after him and take his hand or pick him up and bring him back; he needs physical contact to understand what you mean.

Don't expect a Toddler-Two to share his toys with other children. At this point in his life, his most important developmental task is to find out that he can have some control over himself and his world. Forcing him to share his precious possessions only undermines his feelings of autonomy (self-control) and competence.

Do have two of everything if you have two Toddler-Twos together. Ask your friends to bring their own toys if they come to visit. This applies especially if there are two children in this stage in the same family. They each need their own things so they will be ready to share later on.

Don't expect Toddler-Twos to play happily together. This is the stage of solitary (alone) play and, as he moves toward three, parallel play (beside each other). Cooperative play comes sometime after three.

Do find a five- or six-year-old who will gladly share as a playmate. Older children are not in competition with the Toddler-Two and can play happily with him.

Don't expect a Toddler-Two to dress himself. There may be times when he wants to, but if he doesn't, pitch in and happily help him without belittling.

Do make it a game; you put on one sock and he puts on the other. Self-help will come much faster with a boost from you here and there.

Don't expect a Toddler-Two to pick up his toys all by himself. He needs your help and a pat on the back when he does a little bit.

Do make it a game. "I'll pick up these and you pick up those," or use a timer and see if he can pick up so many by the time it dings.

Don't expect a Toddler-Two to be patient while he is waiting for his meal at the family dinner table or in the restaurant. They are movers and will rebel if confined too closely.

Do have something for him to munch on or some toy to entertain him while he has to wait. If the family dinner table is too distracting for the young child, feed him first, by himself, so he gets what he needs and doesn't keep things in an uproar.

If we don't expect more than a small child can deliver, we save him and ourselves a lot of frustration and disappointment. Expecting too much puts him down and tramples his self-esteem. What he needs most at this age is to feel BIG.

Dr. Jean M. Larsen, supervising graduate students at Brigham Young University in Utah in 1979, has produced a guide to assist parents in developing positive self-concept (high self-esteem) in young children. After 300 preschool children were screened for this study, this procedure for teaching any kind of task to a child was developed:

1. Model, or demonstrate, the task and use a positive statement about what you are doing.

The toys need to be put away. Parent can put some toys in box and say, "I am putting your blocks in this box. I feel good when all the toys are put away."

2. Instruct the child about the task and guide him to a successful completion of it.

Say, "It's your turn to put the toys in the box. Put your blocks in the toy box."

3. Use positive statements of encouragement and acceptance of the child.

Say, "You can put your toys away! I enjoy having you put the toys away with me."

4. Encourage a positive self-statement by the child.

Ask, "How does it make you feel when everything is put away?" Child will reply, "I can do it!" or "I'm a big boy!" You say, "What a big boy!"

This is a skill to be learned by a parent just as using positive commands is. It works to keep everyone happy.

Surviving with the Three- to Five-year-olds

From the third to the fifth year, the child needs to learn "I will."

The Three-to-Five is in the initiative stage where he is learning to refine his skills of self-direction and self-control. Three is a year of equilibrium after the stormy Twos. He is more self-sufficient, usually co-operative, much easier to live with, and just beginning to make decisions and judgments about his own life.

Threes are full of bright ideas; they initiate all kinds of projects, some of which make no sense to you. Here again, if they aren't injurious to your child's health or safety, go along with it as much as you can. He is now beginning to do things for a reason. He has a plan that he will work very hard to complete.

Until now you could select his clothes and he would accept it, but suddenly he wants to use his ideas and wear the red shirt and the yellow sweater and the worn-out pants and fights like a tiger to have it his way. It doesn't really matter to us what he wears, but it matters a great deal to him when we accept his ideas. If we tromp on his ideas, he soon quits trying, and we've killed what we want most for him—the initiative to do his own thinking and planning.

The dinner table can be a real hassle at this age if we don't understand his need to try his own ideas. Your child comes to the table, and he doesn't want the white glass; he wants the blue one. He wants the plate with the duck on it. So he has an idea! It doesn't matter that much, so go along with his idea. This is also a continuing push for autonomy. Better yet, plan ahead and ask him which plate and glass he'd like tonight and avoid the ruckus.

I've observed parents who dictate how and what a child should eat, not allowing him any freedom in this three-times-a-day routine. This is a problem that goes much deeper than eating. When the child sits down to the table, with probably twice as much food on his plate as he needs or wants and a full eight-ounce glass of milk he's ready to eat. As he reaches for the milk, he is told, "Don't drink your milk. Eat your meat first. Eat your vegetable before you eat your bread. Now drink only a little bit of your milk." By this time he's so frustrated he just sits, and then the usual climax—"If you don't eat your dinner, you can't have any dessert." By this time he's lost all interest in food and is sent from the table without it.

Remember, a child will eat what he needs if you provide a balanced diet and allow him to eat it in any order he chooses. Give him a tablespoonful of each kind of food and he can have more if he wants

it. Give him a three- or four-ounce glass of milk and
he can have more if he wants it. The only limit you
put on a child at the table is the choice of sitting up
and eating his meal or leaving the table. Not "If you
don't eat, you'll go to your room," but "Which do you
choose to do—eat your dinner or leave the table?"
or "Have you had enough dinner?" I am concerned
that more good creative initiative is destroyed at the
dinner table than in any other situation, and when it
happens three times a day, it really destroys initiative.

T 'mmy's parents really loved him and thought that
what they wanted for him was best for him. He was
fairly secure in his basic trust because he was a
wanted baby and was enjoyed by his parents. As he
moved into autonomy, his no was translated as defiance, and he was forced to do the routine things
with threats and spankings. At two he was expected
to stay in his room until he was dressed. When he
wouldn't stay in bed at night, he was tied in bed
with a harness. His parents are doers with many
projects, so Tommy was put off and brushed aside
because they were too busy.

As he moved into initiative, he had lots of ideas
because he was a very intelligent boy. Many of his
ideas were inconvenient or bothersome, so they were
ignored. If his parents were too busy to notice an unacceptable behavior, he got away with it, but the
next time he did it and they saw him, he was pun-
ished. This was so confusing he didn't know what to
depend on. Their dinner table was the routine I have
described—"Eat or you get the wooden spoon."

When Tommy entered kindergarten, he didn't

function. When the children were given directions, it was as though he hadn't heard them. After all, he'd never been asked to do anything in a calm and pleasant tone. Only when he was threatened did he move. Tommy is eight now. He has been in a special education classroom with close individual attention from the teachers. He can read, knows his arithmetic factors, and can figure out the most complicated mechanical projects, but he will not assume the responsibility for doing his own schoolwork. At this point the psychologist classifies him as a gifted child who does not perform.

When you take everything out of a child's hands, you kill his initiative. If you use reward and punishment as your motivator, you rob him of self-motivation. Tommy's parents are really trying to modify their methods and to learn to respect this child as a person with an unusual intellect that he needs to be allowed to use. Loving guidance and undivided attention should help build his self-esteem so he will assume responsibility for his life.

The attitudes a child establishes at two and three in completing a task, such as finishing a puzzle (with help if he needs it), picking up his toys (with help), and ordering his belongings, determines his potential to work and achieve in school and later in his work. Work attitudes begin in play.

The Three-to-Five is ready to share in some duties around home like putting the silver on the table, carrying out the trash, and helping sort the laundry. Do not tell him he is a "good boy" when he does what you want him to. That is a judgment and implies that if he does not do what you ask, he is not good. Better to say he is helpful or that you appreciate his cooperation. "I really appreciate your help." He really wants to please you, so give him lots of encouragement.

He should now begin to progress from obedience in the presence of authority to obedience in the absence of authority. This is the development of a conscience (self-control). He will begin to internalize (take as his own) the behavior and values of a model. If he loves you, he wants to be like you, so he begins to copy what you do and say. The way you respond to all situations is the way he will learn to respond. If you are a kind and compassionate person, he will learn kindness and compassion for you and for others. If you are honest, he will learn to be honest.

Now he begins to identify with the male or female role by copying a model (his father or her mother). He practices this in his play with boy-play and girl-play—"You be the mother and I'll be the father." Reflect their pride in being a boy or girl to encourage sex identification.

About his third birthday he needs other children to play with some of the time. As a Toddler-Two, he needed his mother, but at three he needs and enjoys cooperative play with other Threes and Fours. If you don't have a child or two in your neighborhood who is the right age, invite a friend to bring her child to spend the morning, or trade baby-sitting so your child has a playmate. His good social development is dependent on his association with other children as old or older than he is.

Two mornings a week at a good nursery school is

a very valuable experience for any child three years old or older. Only by playing with other children can he learn the social behavior he needs for school success and for his ongoing life with people.

What does a mother look for in choosing a nursery school? On pages 107–110, I have described the philosophies of early learning. Look for the responsive environment with teachers who really care about children. A cooperative (where mothers take turns helping) can be a good experience for mother and child, and less expensive than full care.

Social and emotional adjustment are the important tasks of nursery school. Learning to read can come later.

About age three, or a little later, a child forms an opposite sex attachment to his parents. This is his first attempt to establish a safe romantic relationship.

We don't get upset when a little girl clings to her daddy. In fact, we view it as a good sign that she will be attractive to men. But when a boy hides behind his mother's skirts and shows definite preference for her company, Dad may feel rejected and call him a sissy.

If we understand that this is a normal and necessary development, we will accept this behavior and make children feel good about being a boy and being a girl. Dad could say, "I don't blame you for loving your mother. I love her too."

About three the child who has come through autonomy feeling capable and competent knows he *is* someone. He now uses this knowledge to manipulate his world.

My criterion for behavior is this: Would this be

acceptable in the outside world of nursery school and Sunday school? with friends? later in school with classmates?

Whining is an example. A child wants something (maybe your attention), and he keeps on whining until you give in to him. This will not be tolerated in any group he belongs to, and since you are training him to function in the outside world, you need to nip it in the bud. Don't give in and he will give up!

Sassiness is another trick every child tries. I mean rude, angry backtalk. Allowing this to go on breeds disrespect for you and all other authority figures, especially teachers.

When he tries sassing, grasp him firmly by both shoulders, get down where you can look him directly in the eyes, and say, "You may not talk to me that way. Go sit on that chair until you can think of a better way to tell me how you feel."

ADDITIONAL READING

Briggs, Dorothy C., *Your Child's Self Esteem,* pp. 97–117, 131–138, 180–198.

Dodson, Fitzhugh, *How to Parent,* pp. 155–202.

Hymes, James L., Jr., *The Child Under Six,* pp. 166–191.

Survival Hints for Three-to-Fives

ACCEPTING AND REFLECTING FEELINGS

Since the developmental task of the Three is to work out his initiative, he hangs on to his ideas in spite of everybody. He no longer can be easily distracted, so we need to use another skill to move him when he is so determined.

Accepting and reflecting his feelings helps build cooperation. You call him in from play, but he doesn't want to come. Rather than forcing him (which only makes him fight harder), try reflecting his feelings. "You really don't want to come in, do you? I know you're having fun, but lunch is ready and you *need* to come. I'll race you to the house."

The need of a Three is to be *bigger*. Give him a chance to do jobs that have real meaning. When you go to the store, let him pick some of the groceries off the shelves. He can now make his bed, either with your help or the best he can do on his own (accept whatever he does as a good try). He can now work with you to pick up and organize his own room.

ALLOWING CHOICES

Threes should be allowed to choose what they will wear. You will need to lay out two appropriate outfits, and he can choose which he wants to wear. When you are buying new clothes, choose three in your price range and let him make his choice.

Threes can be moved along by giving choices. Be sure they are legitimate choices. It is time for his nap and he is stalling, so you say, "After you are in bed, I will either read you a story or work a puzzle with you. Which would you like?"

"But I don't want a nap." At this point you say, "You *need* a rest. Would you like the story or the puzzle?" Usually they make the choice and the conflict is resolved.

Avoid a confrontation if you can—nobody wins a confrontation.

You have worked hard to make a good dinner. Your Three comes to the table and says "*Yuck*, meat loaf." Even if you'd like to hit him, reflect his feelings and say, "You must not be hungry," and go right on eating. He'll go on and eat what is in front of him if you play it down. If he really isn't hungry, he has the choice to leave the table.

What do you do when he wants to eat later? Say, "You chose not to eat your dinner, but you may have half a glass of milk before you go to bed." No long lecture—he'll get the message.

A good sense of humor goes a long way to avoid

trouble. Joke about it, kid them out of it, and laugh a lot, and you can enjoy them more.

It helps a great deal if we cut the world down to size for the young child. He will feel bigger and be able to do more things for himself if you—

• Have a step stool at the washbowl so he can reach the water and soap.
• Install low hooks in his closet to hang his clothes on.
• Drop the hanger bar in his closet so he can reach the clothes on hangers.
• Make shelves in his room or family room. Boards on bricks will do. Put his many-piece games in shoe boxes or three-pound coffee cans so he takes only one or two kinds out at a time. Nothing discourages play like a bushel basket of toy parts dumped on the floor. It's easier for him to put away one box of toys and then get a different one.
• Put a wastebasket in his closet for his dirty clothes; it saves picking them off the floor.

One of the playthings essential for creative play at this age is a set of good wooden blocks. The smaller the child, the larger the blocks should be.

A handy dad can get mill ends of hardwood to sand and wax for building blocks. Be sure they are modular, $2 \times 2, 2 \times 4,$ and $2 \times 8.$

Blocks can be anything for the child from two to

twelve years: houses, garages, airports, fire stations, train tunnels—whatever his imagination calls for.

Another essential item of play equipment is a sandbox. Children will spend more happy time with trucks, pans, cans, spoons, shovels, and buckets in a sand pile than anything you can provide. Here he can do what he wants; he doesn't need constant help (as he gets to three), and he can be happy playing, alone.

Locate it where you can check on him from a window. You'll have sand in the house, but the learning and pleasure he will get from sand play is more than worth the inconvenience.

Each child needs a small chair he can call his own and use where he needs it.

A climbing dome is an excellent piece of equipment. He can climb on it, hang on it, and make a house, a tent, or a fort under it. It doesn't need someone to push like a swing does, so he can play by himself or with several other children.

A play table-and-chair set can provide the play center where you are working. About two he can be taught that he needs to sit at his table for snacks, coloring, peg boards, puzzles, and games. This way you can give him help if he needs it, and it helps with the cleanup. Enthusiastic response to his efforts keeps him learning.

Water play is an important and delightful experience for young children. The infant enjoys the feel and sounds of splashing in his bath. The Toddler-Two loves toys that float in the bath tub or plastic bottles and play dishes he can fill and pour while standing on a stool at the sink. Remember, he's wash and wear, and the hour of happy activity is worth the change of clothes.

During the summer children need a swimsuit and a small plastic swimming pool outside where they can wade, splash, pour, pretend, and stay cool. A hose with a small dribble he can manipulate is like tying him with a rope. He won't put it down as long as the water flows.

Don'ts and Dos for Three-to-Fives

We don't learn anything important from anyone we don't love.

Don't assume that you own another person and that his life is in your hands.

Do allow other people (children, spouses) to be separate persons with their own ideas.

Don't insist that teaching the right things is your most important job in life.

Do create a good relationship. Treat your family like you treat your friends.

Don't set such high standards for your child that he gives up trying.

Do base your expectations on your child's ability rather than on your vanity to shine through your children.

Don't expect wrong behavior—either by words or unexpressed feelings.

Do assume a child will do the right thing. He will try to match his performance to your expectations.

Don't compare children or play favorites.

Do help each child to excel in his own unique domain.

Don't live on the double standard of "Do as I say, not as I do."

Do the things you expect of your children. They learn by copying a model more than by lectures.

Don't dwell on a child's shortcomings or see him only as you wish he would be.

Do accept him as he is. Encourage every step, however small, in the right direction.

Don't expect perfection.

Do allow chidren to make mistakes and help them to learn from the experience without belittling.

Don't expect immediate or complete achievement all the time.

Do make a positive comment about any new accomplishment.

Don't label children either good or bad. A Dennis will be a menace if you expect it. A "goodie" becomes dependent on approval for survival.

Do look for something acceptable in each child each day and tell him about it.

Don't passively tolerate behavior that annoys or disturbs you and other people.

Do make clear ground rules. Establish behavior limits and follow through on them.

Don't get so bogged down with everyday problems that you lose the game— and the kids.

Do enjoy each child. Plan regular family fun times. It helps to get over the rough spots.

Don't get so busy and involved that you don't have time for your children.

Do spend frequent happy times with each child so he *feels* loved. *Tell* him you love him.

Mother's Self-Esteem and Her Survival

Surviving as a mother and a woman requires constant bolstering of your own self-esteem. Each of us comes through our childhood and adolescence with varying degrees of self-esteem. The way we have been treated has so much to do with the way we feel about ourselves. Maintaining a high self-esteem is a lifelong endeavor for each of us.

The constant complaint of most young mothers is fatigue. I understand it because I had it, my friends had it, and my daughters had it when their children were young. When you're exhausted, your self-esteem disappears. No one will take care of you if you don't take care of yourself. If you don't provide for rejuvenation periodically, you will crumble under the load you have to carry.

Study and understand good nutrition so you eat for health and beauty. Get the rest you need. A short rest after lunch when your children nap will recharge your battery so you can cope with the rest of the day. These are the most demanding years of your life, so leave the dishes and the dust—they never go away—and catch a nap or do something for you because you'll feel better about yourself. When you like yourself, you can like your children.

Remember how happy and confident you were on your honeymoon? The two of you finally alone and together. Declare a "remember when" night once in a while when you and your honey can get a sitter and go have a hamburger together with no demands from children to interrupt your undivided attention for each other. Busy mothers need to remember that fathers need undivided attention on a regular basis. Maybe it can only be a walk around the block, but renewing the honeymoon is a necessary ritual for maintaining high self-esteem.

When housework and children close in on you, plan a day out. Go see a friend so you can bolster each other. Attend a church or YWCA group where you can converse on an adult level. Two- and three-year-old conversation loses its stimulation after so long. Make time for a project, however small, that will bring you some sense of satisfaction and accomplishment. Maybe it's only arranging a fresh bouquet or repotting a plant, but it gives life beauty, and this we need. If you get knocked down by a remark or a slight from husband or friend, your self-esteem hits bottom, and you find your children more annoying than ever. Pick yourself up and do something for you, and you'll be able to go rolling along.

When you like yourself, you can like your children.

For those of you raising your children alone, take time for yourself. Plan time with your friends without your children. Renew your self-esteem so you can cope with all the demands you have to meet.

While you are kept at home with young children, keep these things in mind:

• I can do this job better than anyone else, so I will reap the rewards of my efforts.

• I will keep my interests and talents alive by doing what *I* like to do on a regular basis, if only for a short time.

• I will make the effort to see my friends and neighbors and to belong to a group for my own stimulation. A cooperative baby-sitting arrangement with friends can give me some freedom.

• I will prepare myself to be alone and to make my time alone rewarding and meaningful. (Statistics show that women survive their mates, so learning to be alone is a lifetime project.)

• I will keep reminding myself that I will have forty or more years to do what I want to do after my children become more self-sufficient.

• There are many problems that have no immediate solution. (Growth takes care of many of them. Console yourself with "This, too, shall pass.")

SURVIVING YOUR ANGER

Every parent is a potential child abuser. Facts show that child abusers cover the spectrum of income, education, color, age, sex, and marital status.

When children are so exasperating, how do you handle the anger you feel?

I think it helps if we understand that anger is a secondary emotion. Anger is the result of another emotion. We are hurt, scared, imposed on, made to feel like a failure, frustrated, or disappointed—and then angry.

When a child expresses disdain for food we've prepared for dinner, it makes us angry, but what is really happening is that we are hurt after we've worked so hard to please.

When some behavior of your child (or anyone else) makes you angry, look for the underlying emotion. This is true of your child's anger too. Try to identify his real emotion. "You are really disappointed you can't come with me."

When you are at the end of your rope and you lose control, what does it do to your child? The greatest harm is not the punishment we dish out (unless we batter him) in our exasperation but the helplessness the child feels when the strong adult he was depending on for strength suddenly acts like a child his own age. If we are adult, we are constantly trying to improve our own controls. If we can control ourselves, we can handle our children.

> If we are mature, we are able to put someone else's needs ahead of our own and postpone our present desires for a future good.

So a series of events is triggered by something a child does and we *blow*. What then?

• When a child is a problem to you, try to tell him how it makes you feel instead of yelling and scolding. Instead of "You are a naughty boy for tracking mud on my clean floor!" tell him how it makes you feel. "When you track mud on my clean floor, I feel so upset because I worked for an hour to get it clean." This doesn't put him down, so he is more apt to co-operate, and *your* problem diminishes when your feelings have been expressed.

When a child's (or anyone's) behavior is a problem to you, how do you get him to change his behavior without trampling his self-esteem? The following is an easy model for construction of an "I message" to express the problem:

State the problem in an unblameful manner.	Say how it makes you feel.	Cite the concrete and tangible effect on you.
Examples: When you come to the dinner table with such dirty hands,	I feel very upset	because you are spoiling my dinner.
When you will not get your clothes on,	I feel very nervous	because we will be late for our doctor's appointment.

• Children need to know we have limits and can be warned. "I don't feel very well today, so don't push me too hard." If you never blow up, you aren't real. If you go overboard in a blowup, wait until after the crisis and then let the child know that you lost your cool and are sorry and that he was not entirely to blame.

• When you are very angry, tell your child that you are so upset you will have to cool off before you can deal with the problem. This doesn't put all the burden on his shoulders.

Try to figure out why you are so angry. Look for the primary emotion. Often the child isn't the culprit —only the catalyst.

• Since mental and emotional stress need release, do something physical. Go out on the porch and take fifty deep breaths of fresh air. Walk around the yard or the block, wash the windows, mow the lawn, shovel the snow, pull weeds, or knead bread. Exert yourself so you don't have to take it out on your children.

• A good walk will help, any time of day or any season of the year.

• Meditation and prayer can help regain your perspective and define your goals.

SURVIVING AS A WORKING MOTHER

More and more women are asking, "Do I need to give up my job when I have my baby?" Each mother has to make this decision for herself. My experience tells me that nurturing a child to his full potential with a healthy personality is so important that I cannot risk what someone else might do. If I want him to learn my values and trust my judgment, I need to provide his experiences and guidance. It is the only way I will know what is really happening. This is his foundation for life. I have only one chance to do it well, and I have to live with the results.

> Take care of yourself and you can cope with your children.

Whether you are working by choice or necessity, you need to define your needs and the needs of your child. If there are any choices in the matter, a child whose mother can stay home with him until he is three will really benefit from the continuity in his life.

If he needs to be cared for by someone else, look at the personality and attitude toward children of the teacher or mother, as well as any program facilities and equipment she provides.

Five o'clock is a very difficult time for a working mother. You've spent your best energy before you get home, and there is so much to be done. Because your child hasn't seen you all day, he can be very demanding.

A flexible schedule can help. While you are preparing dinner, set up a game, a puzzle, crayons, or cutting pictures out of magazines at a counter or play table near you. This is good conversation time.

Right after dinner (the sooner you give undivided attention, the sooner you can get on with your work) take whatever time you can give comfortably. If a half hour is what you can spare—gladly—tell him you have a half hour to do what he wants to do. Quality of time is more important than quantity of time.

Set the timer and when it dings, expect him to entertain himself until bedtime.

If you allow a child to demand all your time in the evening, your feelings of irritation do him more harm than a shorter time gladly given.

At bedtime take additional time for a story.

More undivided attention with time limits, as needed, helps him to be less demanding of you and relieves your guilt feelings for having to be away from him.

Keep in mind that only you can build your relationship with your child. Without a good relationship we have little influence.

New research shows that a child in good quality day care is not damaged by the experience *if* he has a loving, trusting relationship with his mother and father in his home.

ADDITIONAL READING

Briggs, Dorothy C., *Your Child's Self Esteem*, pp. 199–208; 285–304.

Dodson, Fitzhugh, *How to Parent*, pp. 31–39.

Gordon, Thomas, *Parent Effectiveness Training*, pp. 139–147.

Lindberg, Anne M., *Gift from the Sea*, pp. 21–58.

Your Child's Self-Esteem and His Survival

High self-esteem is the magic word in all learning and happy living. A child's self-esteem, the feeling that he has value and that he is loved and capable, comes from the treatment he receives from the important people in his life, his family. His behavior matches his self-esteem. If his self-esteem is high, he likes himself, and he likes you. He feels confident and wants to cooperate with you. If his self-esteem is low, he will feel that he is no good and there is no use trying. He will become defensive or aggressive, uncooperative, and a general nuisance.

When a child has a problem that is coming out in misbehavior, he has a need that isn't being met. In my experience there is no problem of behavior that cannot be modified or changed by giving that child more undivided attention, which is the two of you involved in a pleasant activity. He has your complete attention and love. Misbehavior is low self-esteem. What he is really asking for is the reassurance that he is important to you, and some special time alone with you will give him that assurance. When he doubts you, he doubts himself. When a child balks at bedtime, a half-hour of undivided attention with a story or a game will satisfy his need to be with you, and then he will be willing to separate and go to sleep.

When a child (or anyone else) has a problem, an easy model for reflective listening is on this order:

Say:

You feel	name the emotion	about the problem

Examples:

You feel	left out	when the kids won't play with you.
You feel	unhappy	when Mommy has to leave you.

> Modify the environment to change unacceptable behavior.

When a child is most unlovable, he is crying out for you to prove you still love him and will give him the strength he does not have. Undivided attention is the magic formula for maintaining high self-esteem.

Danny was the oldest of four children in a "yours,

mine, and ours" family. When the families were com-
bined, there was another boy just his age and a girl
two years younger, and within a year there was a
new baby. At four years old he began to mess his
pants again. His mother was disappointed and
ashamed but didn't know how to handle the problem. I suggested that she arrange some time alone
with Danny. She sent the two older children to a
neighbor and put the baby down for a nap and for
one week she spent one hour a day with Danny doing whatever he chose to do. The next week she came
back to class with a big plate of cookies for the group
and said, "It's magic!" In just one week he had been
able to give up the unacceptable behavior because he
was getting the attention he craved without it.

> Enjoy your child. That tells him more than any-
> thing you can do or say that you love him and
> builds high self-esteem.

SIBLING RIVALRY

Sibling rivalry is the quarreling among children in
a family. It is a necessary activity for hammering out
each individual personality and character. We do
need to be concerned if it becomes malicious and
destructive.

A child who feels he is being slighted or displaced
is more apt to make trouble enough to get his parents' attention. Punishment is better attention than
no attention at all.

The more confident a child is that his parents love

and appreciate him, the less he has to struggle against a rival. The troublemaker is crying out for assurance that he is important to you. Some special activities with him alone can help reassure him.

The family is the testing ground for growth. Learning to live with people comes with defining our space. How much room can I have before I infringe on the space of others? How do my actions affect others? Do they respect my space? How do we adjust our needs to each other?

The squabbles of siblings help establish a standard of behavior, much of it out of earshot and sight of parents.

Parents should allow siblings to solve most of their own differences without interference. You may have to step in to keep them from hurting each other, but parents cannot own all their children's problems. If you do take it upon yourself to settle every dispute, you are denying them the practice they need in solving their own problems and establishing their own relationships.

Home duties and belongings cause a lot of conflict. Sit down with children and list the duties that need to be done. Agree on certain jobs to certain children on a rotating basis; then make a work chart to save arguments. In our family we had pay jobs and love jobs. A special favor was a love job. We all end up working for money, so we can't start too early to teach that a job well done pays off.

Some mothers with two or more children have been successful with color-coding belongings. Each child has a color that is on his toys, his clothes, his eating utensils, and his cupboard and closet. This helps the feeling of ownership and also teaches respect for the property of others.

HELPING TWINS SURVIVE

Having raised twin boys, there are some things I've learned the hard way that might be helpful to mothers of twins.

Ours were fraternal twins and as unlike each other as our other children were. They were handsome, husky, and always the same size.

We made a special point to treat them as individuals, calling them "the boys," never "the twins."

All our children were born in the "Professional" era, when doctors and teachers told mothers that only they knew what was best for children. Because I had a degree in psychology, I heeded their advice. "Don't teach the alphabet; you may interfere with what the schools want to teach." Also, because I had a minor in recreation and had worked in it before marriage, I knew children needed to be busy. I provided much of the learning environment (which I now preach about), not knowing what learnings were being accomplished. I knew children needed all kinds of play, so we provided toys and equipment and read to them regularly.

I now know that lack of language skill is a common problem with twins. Since they always have a playmate, they don't demand to talk to their mother as much as a single child does. Language is the door to learning, so talking *with* children (especially twins) and listening while they talk is a key to reading readiness.

I now know that if I had made the effort to talk to them individually and had played with them separately, they probably wouldn't have had the reading difficulty they did when they started school. I now know that twins should be separated in kindergarten so they cannot be dependent on each other, as they are at home.

Our boys did very well until it was time for second grade. Then the teacher realized that No. 1 (the firstborn) had been doing all the work for No. 2 (the secondborn). Consequently, No. 2 hadn't learned his basic vocabulary, and she warned me not to try to teach him. I now know that at least 50 percent of the children learning to read need phonics to train their visual memory. Since this school used the sight method, one of my two boys (50 percent) could not master the sight method, so he was in trouble.

It was unfortunate for him that our family moved to a new home and school district in the middle of his second grade. At the end of the year, the principal insisted he repeat second grade. That blow, for his brother and all his friends to move up and for him to stay behind, destroyed his self-esteem as far as school was concerned. He struggled to overcome it until he graduated from college and finally beat the system.

Looking back, this taught me that reading is not the end and all of life. We made every effort to give these boys successes in many other endeavors. No. 1 was athletic; No. 2 was musical. They both became expert swimmers, skiers, campers, and hikers and were skilled with their dad's power tools. They learned to fix bikes, motorcycles, and cars. When they were in church activities and scouting, they were in the same grade group so No. 2 could be where he belonged. These social experiences helped them excel as individuals. No. 1 is now an architect in historic preservation working for Building Conservation Technology, Inc., in Washington, D.C. No. 2 is a very successful salesman for a large corporation.

If a child is having reading difficulty, help him excel elsewhere to build his confidence. Most of the reading problems are caused by lack of readiness (not enough preschool stimulation and experience) and the low self-image caused by repeated failures to achieve at home and in the classroom. Lack of maturity can cause problems too.

Now that we know what can bring school success, it is a worthy vocation for a mother to pursue.

ADDITIONAL READING

Briggs, Dorothy C., *Your Child's Self-Esteem*, pp. 2–57; 61–71; 82–88.

Gordon, Thomas, *Parent Effectiveness Training*, pp. 29–94, 103–147.

Surviving the Academic Push

How do I find my way through the maze of opposing philosophies of child development that I read in books and magazines and hear on TV talk shows?

Can you visualize a straight horizontal line? At the far left end we will put the school of thought based on the maturation theory of learning, meaning that a child will do what he should do when he is mature enough to do it. We will provide him with toys and play equipment that he will use when he is ready. This stance is one of "Let it happen." In this school of thought the child determines what will happen. It is an unstructured environment, with no plan for the child to follow.

At the far right end of this horizontal line is the school of thought based on the reinforcement theory of learning, meaning learning takes place when the child gets a favorable response for a task completed correctly. Here the teacher determines what happens by structuring a set task for the child to complete. As the child completes one task successfully, he is given a new task. The "Teach your child to read by age three" people fit in here.

In between these two extremes is a middle ground, which is called the responsive environment theory of early childhood education. It uses some things from the maturation school—trying to judge when a child is ready for a new learning. It also depends on the reinforcement school by giving excited approval of a new accomplishment.

The responsive environment is created when the teacher or mother sets up materials that provide a play situation with no set task and no goals to be completed. As the child experiments with and manipulates materials, he makes his own discoveries and learns new skills with no threat of failure. This is creative learning at its best. The philosophy here is that children learn better with some direction, but they need the freedom to use their own thinking and planning abilities.

Learning to say his numbers and letters before he is five is not his most important learning. To learn that he is a capable and worthy person who is allowed to use his own ideas is what is really important. A positive social-emotional development is the most important need of the young child. If he learns through play that learning is fun, he will be eager to learn more, and reading will come easily. If, however, you pressure a child to learning tasks he isn't interested in or ready for, you risk turning off his love of learning and making him feel like a failure because of your disappointment in him. The way you *treat* your child has more to do with his school readiness than any letters and numbers you teach him. If he is accepted by you as a separate and unique person with his own potential, he can respect himself as a person and he can thrive and grow in the sunshine of your loving concern. *The way he feels about himself is the key to all learning, and your attitude toward him determines how he feels about himself.* Try not to get bogged down with the everyday crises. Children are small for such a short time, so don't miss the fun of their spontaneous enthusiasm as they grow and learn.

As you are, I once was.
As I am, you will be.

You have an older child or two and you didn't know these things. All is not lost. If you missed or "messed up" any of the developmental tasks with a child, go back and make them up—at any age.

Building basic trust is a life-long job. Work to develop a warm relationship with each child by giving him your undivided attention in pleasant activities. When he feels loved because you give him your time, he will strive harder in school and life.

If you squashed his autonomy, give him more responsibility in meaningful jobs so he can feel capable. Always be willing to help him. Give him a pat on the back for any part of a job well done.

If he is having difficulty in school, ask his teacher to get an older pupil to help him.

Include him in the decisions that affect his life —sharing power, allowing choices, and reflecting feelings.

The High/Scope Educational Research Foundation has been conducting a long-term experiment to determine the effects of quality preschool education. Now there is solid evidence that quality preschool experience *does* help reduce society's problems.

Following a group of children until they are fifteen years old shows that more of the children who had preschool experiences have

1. a stronger commitment to school and to doing well in school

.2. higher scores in reading, language, and arithmetic at all grade levels

3. a 50 percent reduction in the need for special education through high school

4. less tendency to display antisocial and delinquent behavior outside school

5. after-school jobs and plans for college.

Another important finding of this research shows that a child learns faster and better when the mother participates in and supports the program, does home task assignments with the child, and exhibits interest in his activities and progress in preschool and throughout school.

Reading Readiness for Survival

A Parent Is the Best Educational Toy of All

With the knowledge we have that children acquire 50 percent of their mental ability by the time they are four and that they have formed their attitude toward learning by the time they are three, mothers shoulder more responsibility for their children's success in school than the schools do.

Dr. Mary B. Lane of San Francisco State University has identified the necessary preschool learning for children as "Precursors of the Academics" (what needs to be learned before reading and writing and arithmetic). I have taken the developments she has identified as necessary and given a number of activities a mother can do with her child in order to encourage these developments.

Remember, intelligence grows with interaction between a child and an adult or another child. Taking time to explore some of these activities with your child is writing an insurance policy for his success in school.

Learning needs to be fun, without the threat of

failure. Take time to plan a play experience for your child before you start your day's work. If he is busy with something interesting to do, you can get your work done. If not, he can be a constant pest. I always suggest that a child about two and a half be provided with a play table and chair so he has some place near where you are working to do his puzzles, color, cut, work his play dough, and use his record player. This way you can be the "help on the fly" that is so important to his progress. He won't stay with anything very long if he's back in his room alone.

Study the suggestions on the following pages and use them for your undivided attention. By doing this on a regular basis, you are stimulating his intellect and nourishing his self-esteem.

TELEVISION

What about television? "Sesame Street" has been a great boon to young children. The preschool population is learning the phonic sounds and some of the precursors that are needed for reading. A recent appraisal of the effect of television carries some warnings. Too much television is teaching the child to watch without paying attention. The biggest complaint of classroom teachers today is that children are "tuned out" to what is going on around them. Research shows that the average child has spent from five to fifteen thousand hours in front of a television set before he enters kindergarten. This means that he has not spent these hours out playing, learning how to do things, developing his own toys, and communicating with other children. Learning is an *action process.* We don't really learn anything we don't participate in. The frightening increases in reading problems may be caused by this passive, uncreative pastime that involves all our children.

If you provide interesting activities for your child, he won't need so much TV.

A child needs the real experience before he can interpret a picture. He needs to talk about and discuss what he sees so we know how much of it he really understands. The language he uses to tell you about what he has seen is the real learning he gets from television. By all means, control what he sees and how much. It may not be as easy as having him entertained a lot, but it will pay dividends when he gets to school.

The only thing you can give a child that no one else can give him is what you give of yourself.

ADDITIONAL READING

Dodson, Fitzhugh, *How to Parent,* pp. 272–299.

I Took His Hand and Followed

My dishes went unwashed today,
I didn't make the bed,
I took his hand and followed
Where his eager footsteps led.

Oh yes, we went adventuring,
My little son and I . . .
Exploring all the great outdoors
Beneath the summer sky.

We waded in a crystal stream,
We wandered through a wood . . .
My kitchen wasn't swept today
But life was gay and good.

We found a cool, sun-dappled glade
And now my small son knows
How Mother Bunny hides her nest,
Where jack-in-the-pulpit grows.

We watched a robin feed her young,
We climbed a sunlit hill . . .
Saw cloud-sheep scamper through the sky,
We plucked a daffodil.

That my house was neglected,
That I didn't brush the stairs,

In twenty years, no one on earth
Will know, or even care.

But that I've helped my little boy
To noble manhood grow,
In twenty years, the whole wide world
May look and see and know.

—Author Unknown

Survival with a Seriously Ill or Handicapped Child

The trauma and heartbreak felt by parents when they are informed that the child they had anticipated with such joy is born with a physical or mental handicap, or when parents of a normal child find out he has a fatal disease, can be understood only by those who have experienced it.

The shock and disbelief that this could be happening to us and the repeated questioning of why, why, leaves us confused and bewildered because we know nothing about the problem or the treatment.

Many hospitals have trained social workers and volunteer parents who can help the family step by step with the anxiety of the constant crises that suddenly face us. Dealing with the feelings of disappointment, the bewilderment, and the overwhelming responsibility is a very important step in facing up to and learning to live with what is happening.

We need to understand that the feelings of disappointment and sometimes embarrassment with a special child are normal. Of course, there are deep hurts, and unless we can talk about and deal with these feelings, we may develop defensive attitudes. These attitudes then interfere with our progress in helping our child. Healthy attitudes are essential because the abnormal then becomes normal, and the child does not suffer because of defensiveness on our part.

Finding out the exact cause of the problem as soon as possible can relieve any guilt feelings we have that it may' have been caused by something *we* did or did not do.

Social workers usually warn that the emotional, physical, and financial demands of a sick or handicapped child can put relentless stress on a marriage. The mother may feel that the father could be more help. Father may feel that his wife doesn't care about his need for attention and affection and may feel displaced. Financial worries can be a big source of tension in a family faced with huge medical and therapy bills.

All these feelings start small and become mountains unless they are brought out and recognized as natural reactions of parents facing these problems. A social worker can be very helpful for open and frank discussions of these deep fears and frustrations because an outside person can be objective and point out all sides of the dilemma based on training and experience.

Sometimes the feelings of disappointment interfere with building a warm and loving relationship with our child. They may make it difficult to show the attention needed for any child to feel loved and accepted so he can learn and grow.

The anxiety that parents feel when they look to the future of the child with a health problem may manifest itself in overprotective treatment, which makes the child too dependent on them. Every child needs to be moved toward independence. When he learns to do things for himself, he feels good about himself and everyone around him.

Other children in the family take on our attitudes. If we accept, they will accept. If we are compassionate, they learn to be compassionate. We do need to find a certain amount of time for special undivided attention for the other children so they don't feel left out.

All parents need to study and understand the developmental stages of growth in young children. Learning what to expect at each stage of emotional, physical, and intellectual development helps to keep our expectations in line with the child's ability to perform. All of the information in this book applies to all children, whether they are normal and healthy or whether they are handicapped, sickly, or seriously ill. Parents of a seriously ill or handicapped child will find it harder to accept the problem behavior as normal for his age and stage of growth, especially in the autonomous (Toddler-Two) stage. They are inclined to see the behavior as a result of his handicap rather than as typical for his age and stage of growth.

Joining with a group of parents who are facing the same problems helps us to cope with ours and may lead to some solutions for us. Sharing our feelings of guilt, hostility, anxiety, and rejection will bring supportive response from parents who have learned to deal with these feelings. Taking positive action helps parents adjust. Seek good medical advice and follow through with recommended therapies, including any home treatment and teaching you can do.

All parents need to plan time when they can be together and renew their own relationship. Special children are such a drain that their parents need this time even more than they did before they had a handicapped child. You need to lead your own lives so you can regain your perspective and count what you have going for you instead of getting bogged down with what you don't have.

We don't know the learning potential of any child, so don't sell your child short. Acceptance, loving interaction, stimulation, a consistent routine, and reasonable limits open the door for learning for each child, beginning at birth.

Get help with therapy and educational skills as soon as possible. All of the stimulation and readiness activities in this book can be helpful to any child. Also, there are many therapeutic programs available for the special child from birth to three. Formal education can start at three and continue through age twenty-one.

What about discipline? Establishing ground rules and setting limits are just as important for the special child as for any other child. Learning to live in the real world with good self-control and as much independence as possible builds self-esteem.

The child learns to like himself by being capable of doing things for himself. It takes time, patience, and consistency. Give your child a chance to try Expect everything and he will be more likely to respond because he wants to please you. It is realistic to expect certain things. Drill it in. He can learn. Excited responses from his family for each small accomplishment moves him ahead. Each thing he learns opens the door to more learning and more independence.

Great strides are being made for the welfare of handicapped and seriously ill children because parents have organized and are being heard.

Parents of seriously ill or handicapped children should ask their doctors to direct them to other parents or parent groups who are learning to cope with similar problems.

The national information center for children with handicaps is

Closer Look
Box 1492
Washington, D.C. 20013

Infant and Toddler Stimulation

• Birth to six weeks. Put your baby on his stomach several times a day to encourage lifting his head. Get his attention by talking to him.

• Eight to ten weeks. Hold a bright rubber toy or ball where he can follow it with his eyes. Encourage him to reach for it. Touch his cheek to make him smile. As you hand him food, a spoon, or a toy, make him reach for it. This encourages eye-hand coordination. A Cradle Gym in his crib will encourage activity. A mirror hung over his crib 8 to 10 inches above his eyes will help him see himself. As he grows older, say his name. Teach him to identify his eyes, ears, nose, and so on.

• Four to ten months. Provide space for baby to crawl. Learning to crawl is very necessary for his physical and intellectual development. If you confine him to a playpen, you handicap his growth. Every mother needs a playpen for the times during the day when she needs to do her work. Every child needs to learn to entertain himself for short periods of time. A schedule of an hour in the playpen and equal time to crawl and explore benefits both mother and child.

• The age-old rhythm verses help teach language: Peek-a-boo, Pat-a-cake, This Little Pig Went to Market, So Big. The more action you put in it, the better he'll like it.

• Nesting cans. Coffee cans have smooth plastic tops and no sharp edges if a can opener that trims the edges has been used. So use a three-pound, two-pound, one-pound and a half-pound can to make a good set of nesting, stacking toys. A hole in the plastic lids provides a good "drop-in" toy, using large beads or poker chips. Stacking cones are good toys too.

• The Toddler enjoys screwing lids on bottles. A variety of plastic bottles will keep him busy.

• Rolling balls of all sizes to a Toddler who is sitting on the floor will delight him.

• Pulling pans and bowls out of the cupboard to stack and manipulate provides endless pleasure. Accepting this as a learning experience instead of a mess tells him you approve of his curiosity, the key to learning.

• A Toddler throwing toys out of his crib or dropping things from his high chair is playing the game of "What happens when . . ." Join the fun.

• Start reading picture books to him at about ten months. Linen books that he can look at by himself will not tear. The new small books with stiff pages satisfy his need to see how hinges work. Turning the pages is more interesting to him than the story.

• Talk to your child the day he is born. The rhythm

and sound of your voice is relating and stimulating long before he can understand what you are saying. Talking with him, reading to him, and playing with him are the interactions he needs to develop physically, emotionally, and intellectually. He'll be able to follow directions and commands long before he can talk. He needs an enthusiastic audience when he is learning language, so be a cheerful listener.

• Infant seats are very convenient, but be careful not to use them too much. A hard, plastic carrier is a poor substitute for the warmth of a mother's arm.

Talking About Pictures

One of the easiest and most convenient ways to learn many of the skills needed for reading is talking about pictures. A child as young as six months will sit while his mother turns pages of magazines and names the objects and people they see. This is the first step in building vocabulary. Children enjoy the rhythm and sound of words long before they know the meanings. As you read stories or post a picture on the refrigerator door, help him see these things, talk about them, and enjoy them.

Visual Discrimination

Point out likenesses and differences in the picture—all the boys, all the girls, houses, trees, boats, and so on.

Help him see various shapes and sizes. Which is larger? Are there two alike? How many small ones are there?

He will need to be able to pick out figures from the background, so identifying people and objects in a picture is good practice.

Talk about colors. Pick out all the red objects. How many green trees? If he says the wrong color, just say the correct one without pointing out his error.

Count objects and people in any picture. He needs to count objects before he is ready to learn the symbol for the number.

Spatial Relationships

The ability to tell the differences in letters and words on the printed page comes from seeing differences in positions of things around us and in pictures and books.

Talk about the position of things. Which is on top? Is it in front or in back? inside or outside? above or below? What is in the middle of the picture? What is at the top? on the bottom?

Talk about right and left. Follow the story by pointing out the words from left to right as you read. Is the dog on the left or right of the picture?

Language Development

What do you think is happening in this picture?

Can you make up your own story about it?

You make up a line and I'll make up one to tell a story.

What would happen if . . . ?

Concept Development

Can you tell if it is warm or cold weather?

Is it a happy picture? How can you tell?

Why do birds build nests in trees?

How would our lives be different without cars?

REMEMBER: Keep it light and keep it happy.
Learning should be *FUN!*

SCRAPBOOKS

Cutting with scissors and pasting are excellent activities in readiness. Give your child several old magazines and let him cut out whatever he wants to. Let him make a scrapbook, using shelf paper or an old loose-leaf binder.

Suggest that he might like to have a page of cars, a page of planes, or dogs or girls or houses. He could have a house book with a page for living room furniture, bedroom items, kitchen furnishings, and so on.

This gives him practice in grouping and classifying, as well as a reason for cutting.

Suggest that he cut out and paste all the pictures of things beginning with the same letter, for example s—shoes, socks, sandwiches, stars, stoves, sweaters.

Boys especially need this kind of activity to develop small muscle skills for writing. They are so apt to play ball all the time.

BEAN-BAGS

Make three bean-bags out of sturdy cotton cloth five inches in diameter—a red square, a yellow circle, and a blue triangle. Fill with the cheapest beans available at the grocery store.

This game is designed to develop the skill necessary to hit the target. This requires eye-hand coordination as well as judgment of distance. In order to help your child understand and evaluate his own efforts, please talk over the effect of his throwing. For instance, when he throws a bean-bag into the container he decorated a week or so ago, say what happens.

"Your bean-bag went inside the basket."
"Your bean-bag went outside the basket."
"Your bean-bag went to the right."
"Your bean-bag went too far to the left."
"Your bean-bag went behind the basket."
"Your bean-bag went in front of the basket."

The following concepts of space relationships are very important for a child to understand before he is ready for the reading-readiness activities of the early school years:

> in front of—in back of
> inside—outside
> in the middle—to the right or left
> on top of—below
> over—under.

In addition to learning about space relationships, your child can practice naming shapes and colors. The bean-bags are round, square, and triangular, as well as red, yellow, or blue.

COOKING

Helping Mommy cook is a fun learning experience for the Three- to Five-year-old. The amount of it you can do will depend on the kind of person you are. If you can't stand a mess, don't try it. Working near you and observing what you're doing is teaching with real work.

As you talk about what you're doing, they learn these things: new vocabulary; following directions; sequence (what needs to come first, next, and so on); that ideas come from books; measuring (whole, half, and so on); keeping time by watching the clock to see when it's finished; and seeing changes in ingredients when they are mixed, cooked, or cooled.

They will enjoy making Jell-O, instant pudding, soup, and sandwiches. Cookies for special holidays are a memorable experience. Give your child a ball of dough and let him make his own creations.

Motor Development

In early childhood the mental and physical are closely related; motor activities play a major role in intellectual development.

Exploring, touching, manipulating, throwing, pushing, pulling, and experimenting are crucial in the child's development. If you limit him to a playpen, you rob him of his most valuable learning experiences.

Ability to Determine Left and Right

The child needs to know that he is the center of his world. The development of laterality is extremely important, since it permits us to keep things straight in the world around us. Confusion of *b* and *d* in reading is lack of this development.

As he is being dressed, say, "Right shoe, left shoe."

Show me your right foot, hand, ear.

Shake your right foot, hand.

Look in the left-hand drawer.

Hold my right hand with your left hand.

Which side do the spoons go on the table?

Where does the knife go? Where does the fork go?
Which side of the street do we drive on?

Identify Body Parts

A child's body is his most important possession. He
needs to know it and be proud of it.

Name his own body parts.

Use a mirror sometimes so he can see himself.

Identify body parts in pictures.

Name the body parts in the pictures he draws.

Eye-Hand Coordination

The development of eye-hand coordination is a
prerequisite for the learning of writing and reading.
These things help:

Mobiles in the crib.

Objects to reach and grasp.

Bathtub toys, kitchen utensils, screw tops, blocks,
stacking toys.

Pegboards, puzzles, card-lacing, embroidery, play
dough.

Story board (9″ x 9″ board with nails every inch both
ways). Have him stretch colored rubber bands between
nails to make a design. Let him tell about it.

Large wooden or plastic beads for stringing, empty
spools, detergent bottle caps, large macaroni, popcorn.

Scissors, crayons, pencils, paste, paints, and brushes.

Dot pictures—follow the dots.

Show shapes, circles, squares, and so on, "Draw one
like this."

Make 2½″ x 4″ cards with lowercase letters. Let him copy them.

Show him the letters in his name. Always teach lowercase (small) letters first. Use capital letters to begin his name. When he wants to write his name, have him start at the upper left-hand corner of the paper; otherwise he may write it backward.

Throwing and catching bean-bags, large and small balls.

Balance

The development of balance is very closely related to thinking processes.

Large cardboard box blocks (made by stuffing with newspapers and taping tightly) to stack, stand on, and jump off of.

Balance beam 2″ x 4″ x 8′. Start with 4″ side, 2″ side later.

Walk curbs, climb trees, ladders, climbing bars.

Junglegyms, slides, swings.

Bongo board, twist board.

Tricycle, bicycle, scooter, skate board, roller skates.

What is your child's level of motor development by the time he starts kindergarten?

Can he hop on the right foot? left foot? Can he skip?

Can he throw a bean-bag or ball and hit a target? Can he catch a tossed ball?

Using sidewalk lines, can he walk the line and keep his balance?

Can he walk a balance beam, hands out straight? hands on hips?

Can he tie his shoes, zip his zippers, button his clothes, and put on and fasten his boots?

Can he cut with scissors and use pencils, crayons, paste, and paints?

Perceptual Development

Reading readiness requires many skills in understanding the world your child sees, hears, and touches. He needs to be able to see differences and likenesses in shape, line, size, position, and figure-ground. *Figure-ground* is a term that relates to the perception of a figure in relation to its background. For example, a child bouncing a ball outdoors focuses his attention on the ball (figure) without being distracted by the sidewalk, nearby trees, bushes, and other objects in his surroundings (ground).

Visual Discrimination

As you read stories or look at pictures in magazines or post a picture or make up different projects, do this:

Ask questions to help child distinguish big-little, larger-smaller, short-tall, alike-different, and how many.

Ask child to match geometric forms. Give him a large card with circles, triangles, squares, diamonds, and rectangles on it and give him small forms to match.

Ask child to look at pictures or designs and pick out the main figure, recurring designs, and people from the background. This helps develop figure-ground perception, which is a skill needed in learning to read.

Have child sort buttons into sections of an egg carton to group all that are alike.

Ask child to sort colored cards or disks to find all alike.

Provide playing cards or Old Maid cards and have child sort them.

Find and cut out various letters in magazines and newspapers. Have child match and differentiate.

Spatial Perceptions

The ability to differentiate *b* and *d* depends on the perception of spatial relationships. As you read stories, travel in the car, and work around home, note the position of everything: above, below, inside, outside, in front of, behind, on top of, under, right side, and left side.

Use blocks or toy cars to suggest beside, on top of, and so on.

Use two pegboards and golf tees. Make a design and have child copy it. Put in different numbers of tees and have child match yours.

Give child commands to follow: "Look under your bed." "Look inside your toy box." "Put it on the top shelf."

Whole-part Concepts

Use puzzles, measuring cups, and take-apart toys.

Make cardboard with a circle and square on it; make same size circle and square on colored paper; cut into

¼, ½ and ⅓ sections and have child match to cardboard circle and square.

Classification and Grouping

As you read illustrated stories, find all the girls, boys, cows, houses, and so on.

Using colored beads or several kinds of dry beans or different kinds of macaroni, let your child put like kinds in cups or sections of egg cartons.

Use animal picture cards; have him sort to find alikes.

Play card games like Old Maid and Walt Disney or use regular cards, grouping color and suits and numbers.

Cut pictures out of magazines and make a scrapbook with like kinds on a page—houses, cars, flowers, animals, boys, girls, men, and women.

Use dice or dominoes to find dot groupings.

Find with child all the red things in the room; find all the living things in the room.

Match letters and numbers that are the same.

Visual Memory

Show card with shape, number, letter, or design; child tries to draw what he has seen after model had been covered. Increase difficulty of concepts as he learns.

Place five or six objects on a table; have him turn away and name what he saw.

Touch a series of things around the room; have him name them in order.

An excellent game for training visual memory is "I'm

going to Grandma's and I'm going to take an airplane."
The second person repeats the sentence and adds an
item that starts with *b*—"I'm going to Grandma's and
I'm taking an airplane and a balloon." The third person
says, "I'm going to Grandma's and I'm taking an airplane, a balloon, and a cat." Go around the group as
many times as it takes to include all the alphabet. This
is a good travel or campfire game.

Language Development

Language is learned by copying a model. Correct child's speech by repeating his sentence correctly *without* pointing out his mistakes. Hearing and speaking language precedes thinking, so be courteous in your listening. Allow him lots of practice in speaking and listening to develop his thinking.

Talk to your child from the day he is born.

Sing songs and say rhymes.

Name the parts of his body as you dress him.

Name things you hand to him and feed him. Later he will repeat them.

Talk about the things in his world: animals, cars, people, toys, and household objects and tasks.

Read stories beginning at ten months. Name objects, tell of actions, and so on.

Read traffic signs and name objects and activities as you travel; count horses, gas stations, and so on.

Teach as you shop: name products, colors, shapes; tell him what you will make out of what you buy. Read labels so he hears what they say.

Play recordings; they are excellent language experiences.

Listen to and encourage him to describe his everyday experiences. Be a good listener.

Enjoy jokes, puns, and riddles with him.

Read labels, menus, and directions for games.

Use TV programs as springboards for discussion and understanding.

Read to him regularly to increase his span of attention and vocabulary.

Play games to encourage the use of language. All games are helpful.

Phonics. Hearing the differences in sounds of letters and pronunciation of letters can be encouraged by careful speech of those around him. Pick out the sounds (not the names) of the letters as you read and speak, for example, "Mother starts with *mmm.*" Teach the sounds of letters first. Names of the alphabet letters will come from nursery songs, rhymes, and so on. Some letters have more than one sound:

a says *at, ate, all*

e says *egg, she*

i says *kit, kite*

o says *off, go, do*

u says *up, use, push*

c says "s" when followed by *e, i* or *y*

g says "j" when followed by *e, i* or *y*

s may say "s" as in *six* or
          "z" as in *exercise*

Make a set of 2½ × 4½-inch cards with letters 1 inch high. Use small letters first (lowercase). Capital letters can be introduced as the first letter in child's name.

Leave cards on his play table, where he can experiment with the letters, saying them, copying them, matching them, and so on.

Make a Bingo game with letters on small squares. Call out *sounds* and cover a large Bingo card. Point out beginning sounds of names of objects around the room.

Activities That Help Develop a Meaningful Vocabulary

Describe pictures of all kinds.

Visit school, stores, fire station, zoo, park, dairy, and bakery.

Tell stories with bag puppets or finger puppets.

Play telephones, make-believe, housekeeping, and dress-up play.

Ask questions about familiar objects and situations:
What is the boy doing? Where is he? How does he feel? What will he do if . . .? What will he do next?

Rote teach poems, nursery rhymes, songs, and nonsense verses.

Explain and describe needs and experiences.

Adequate language skill helps a child control his behavior. He needs to learn to ask for what he wants in clear language. If he is having problems with another child, or you, and he is hitting, biting, or pushing, say to him, "*Tell* him what you want instead of hitting him. *Tell* him to move instead of pushing him."

This should be learned with the close supervision of an adult when a child is two to four.

Record some favorite stories on cassette tapes. Your child can entertain himself when you're busy, or you can take them in the car when traveling.

Conceptual Development

Conceptual thinking grows out of experience that can be recalled and reproduced. A child who has seen a camel at the zoo can recognize the picture of a camel in a book. He can draw a camel from his visual image of a camel. We help furnish these images by giving the child many experiences.

Seeing real animals at the zoo or on a farm.

Seeing and riding on buses, trains, planes, boats, and in cars.

Visiting the airport, train depot, and docks.

Identifying community helpers and how they make our life more pleasant: postmen, milkmen, firemen, policemen, nurses, doctors, teachers, ministers, and garbage men.

Encouraging dramatic play to help him understand their jobs.

Identifying the people who make our food, clothing, and shelter: grocer, butcher, builder, dressmaker, bricklayer, and so on.

Television furnishes many images that need explanation because they are beyond the child's understanding and experience.

The concept of time comes with talking about time—about hours, days of the week, months of the year, yesterday, tomorrow, a long time ago, a birthday, vacation time, when Grandma was a child, and museums.

The concept of direction and maps can be taught with:

Asking where the sun comes up and goes down.

Sharing map while traveling to clarify direction.

Allowing child to arrange his own room; make a map of it.

Making a map of his house floor plan.

Making a map of his route to school, church, or the grocery store.

Identifying locations of news events on a map.

Number concepts are learned by:

Counting objects, people, animals, birthdays.

Providing an egg carton numbered 1 to 9 with beans to match numbers.

Making 2½″ x 4½″ cards and printing numbers on them to teach the symbols for the numbers.

Matching card numbers with beans, Popsicle sticks, or toothpicks.

Using imprinted cards as models for writing numbers.

Reading a thermometer to judge what wraps to wear.

Playing games that count spaces, dots, objects: dominoes, checkers, Old Maid, Fish, Hearts, Ropes and Ladders, Monopoly.

Counting money: pennies, nickels, dimes, quarters.

Problem-solving requires conceptual thinking. Practice in problem-solving can be gained by:

Games of all kinds that require counting, matching suits, and matching numbers, letters, and pictures.

Puzzles, put-together toys, blocks.

Making decisions is learned with practice. Give children a choice as often as possible.

"Do you want to wear your coat or sweater?"

"Would you like to go with me or stay with Daddy?"

"Do you want to take a nap or go to bed early?"

All kinds of creative activity require choice and decision. Provide paper, scissors, pencils, crayons, clay, colored paper, paints, scraps of cloth, and blocks.

The development of balance is closely related to conceptual development. A good sense of balance also develops the control needed for writing and reading. Children need to climb, walk lines, walk curbs, walk a balance beam, play on Junglegyms, throw and catch balls, ride scooters, use skate boards, and swim.

Cognitive Development

Cognitive learning includes everything we perceive (see, hear, touch, smell, and taste) and everything we know about our environment. Since the senses of taste and touch are the first to develop in an infant, the tender loving touching by Mother is one of the child's most important learnings. Skin contacts are the sole means of communicating security and affection, a need more important than the feeding process. What a child feels in his first six months of life, from all his senses, will have its greatest impact on his evolving personality and physical development.

Learning to Observe

The senses of a child are very sharp because everything is new. He can be helped to develop them.

Cultivate an awareness of the world around him; make note of the weather, the temperature, the clouds, the stars, the bugs, the birds.

Develop his sense of *feel* by pointing out soft fur, scratchy sandpaper, smooth Jell-O, cold frozen food, and warm sand.

Listen for soft sounds and loud sounds as you take walks.

Trace the progress of budding trees and shrubs.

Watch birds build nests; visit new offspring at the zoo.

Plant seeds in March in the house in a glass bottle filled with Kleenex; put seeds between wet Kleenex and glass to see root formation; beans, peas, or nasturtium seeds work well.

Place celery in colored water to show how plants take in water. Celery will take up the color.

Illustrate use of magnets, magnifying glass, and prisms.

Comparing Ideas and Information

Encourage child to compare what he observes, noting likenesses and differences in size, shape, number, position, color, and age.

As you read books and magazines—and as he plays with blocks, cars, dolls, and so on—note if something is small, smaller, or smallest.

Is is wide? narrow? half? whole? light? heavy? tall? short? more? less?

How are they alike? How are they different?

Classifying Ideas and Information

Practice in grouping develops the ability to solve problems and organize ideas. Here are things you can do to help your child.

After you read a story, discuss what comes first, next, and so on.

Group blocks by size or color.

Cut pictures out of magazines; have him group all the

cars, houses, bedroom furniture, tools, outdoor equipment, kitchen equipment, trucks, girls, and boys. A scrapbook with each group on a page is excellent.

Let him help you sort the laundry by kind, by person, and so on.

Help him organize his belongings with drawers or boxes for clothes and toys. Label shelves so he can learn order.

Interpreting, Describing, Sequence, and Recall

Encourage your child to tell you what he is doing and how he is doing it.

Let him make up stories or describe a picture you have posted.

Ask him to tell you what he did on his last birthday.

Encourage him to convey his wishes and needs clearly.

Involve him in your baking so he learns what comes first in making cookies, Jell-O, punch, or pudding.

Find pictures of his daily activities; have him put them in order and describe what he does.

Help him recall things he did yesterday, at Grandma's, or on vacation.

Ability to Attend

A child increases his attention span by having interesting things to do.

Listening to stories, playing games, blocks, puzzles, cutting, pasting, and coloring increase attention span.

Make your own puzzles by pasting a picture on cardboard and cutting it into odd shapes.

If he can play close to where you are working, he can ask questions and visit while he stays with his project.

Creativity

Imagination, curiosity, exploration, invention, and pretending are the basis for creativity.

Point out new and unexpected developments and relationships rather than teaching by rote: What would happen if? What would you add? How would you change it? Could we do it another way?

Encourage him to create his own stories from a picture, imaginary incidents, wishes or dreams.

Allow him complete freedom with crayons and pencils rather than coloring books to fill in. (Occasional use is fun.)

Encourage story telling with the use of paper-bag or finger puppets.

Encourage him to share your own interests and hobbies.

When he uses clay or play dough, provide cookie cutters, tongue depressors, play dishes, small paper plates, spice bottles for rolling pins, and toothpicks.

Have a "make box" filled with colored paper scraps, old Christmas cards, fabric scraps, trimmings, string, cotton, pipe cleaners, buttons, magazine pictures, and Popsicle sticks. These items can be pasted on paper plates or paper to make collages.

Provide large packing boxes or cartons to use as forts, playhouses, spaceships, schools, and so on.

Supply dramatic play props: canned goods and paper bags for playing store; small paper pads, paper punch, and suitcases for playing train; play dishes and table for playing house; a good supply of dress-up clothes.

Tell round robin story. He starts the story, you add something, he adds some, and so on.

Play car games. Count different-colored cars. Think of many uses for a paper cup, a pencil, a brick. "I'm going to Grandmother's and I'm going to take an apple." Next person says an apple and a book, each one repeating all items in alphabetical order.

Another game is to choose a word and think up a list of similar sounds, like *cat-hat,* and so on.

Provide a place where your child can work alone when he wants to. Praise his accomplishments.

Allow a three-year-old to select his own clothes within a group of three you have selected as proper.

A parent who talks happily with a small child and listens seriously in return is helping creativity to grow.

It is a fortunate child, indeed, whose mother sings to him, teaches him songs of all kinds, and provides him with records of songs, stories, and musical games.

Playthings

Some do-it-yourself presents—not always thought of as presents. Many of these things you already may have in your house.

Box of Junk and a Screwdriver (a boy's dream)

> Springs, padlocks and keys, old clocks to take apart, radio parts, pulleys, bits of rope, latches, wheels, basin plugs, door stoppers, zippers, short chains, bunches of keys, marbles, doorknobs, nuts and bolts, paper clips.

Box of Pictures (to paste, look through, sort, cut)

> Pictures from old magazines of food, cars, trains, planes, old valentines, greeting cards, airmail stickers, postcards, bank deposit slips, transfers, coupons, empty stamp books, paper lace doilies, bits of cellophane and foil wrapping. Strips of colored paper child can make rings and chains with. Colored straws. Flat boxes (as stocking boxes) are good with these so child can separate the different items.

Box of Paste, Paste Brush, Scissors, Crayons, Paper and Cardboard (to use with the above)

Flour mixed to a paste with water can be used for paper work if you have no paste in the house.

Box of Scrap Cloth, Felt, Leather, Lace, Feathers, Ribbons, Rickrack, and so on.

Box of Round Clothespins (still available in some stores)

and bits of material to wrap them in. Crayons to make faces and bits of wool to glue as hair.

Boxes of All Kinds of Little Wheels and Spools (will be sorted, built with, painted, strung, and used as wheels)

Spools of all sizes given away by tailors, dressmakers, and garment manufacturers, electrical wire spools by hardware stores and electrical shops, typewriter ribbon spools, cardboard ribbon spools, adhesive tape spools, cores from Scotch tape.

Box of All Kinds of Buttons (for children old enough not to swallow them)

Children will sort these, string them, and treasure them.

Box of Small Shells (to sort, glue, and so on)

Dress-up Clothes

Grown-ups' clothes shortened, men's and women's hats, vests, ties, bags, and shoes; old junk jewelry, scarves, aprons, and so on. Put in a special box or old suitcase.

Old Clean Sheets

(or poncho or tarpaulin) to put over table, chair, or box as a "secret" house, wigwam, or garage. You can sew the sheet into a box shape, but it is not necessary. Children can change it around, crayon on it, paint on it, and glue on it what they want.

Rug Samples, Linoleum Squares, Tiles

Given away at rug or linoleum and tile places. To use for dollhouses or to play with, together with blocks. Many other uses too.

Pipe Cleaners

Used to twist into animals and people, to string spools, and so on. As handles, for Christmas bells made out of egg carton divisions.

Little Note Pads

Come in assorted colors.

Paper Bags, Paper Plates, Paper Cups

To crayon, paint, make hats, masks, and baskets.

Colored Drinking Straws

Box of Band-Aids

Children like to patch up their dolls, animals, and themselves.

Stapler and Staples

Kitchen Tools

Plastic or metal funnels, a small flour sifter, a real egg-beater, wooden spoons.

Digging Tools

For older children, trench shovels from any army surplus store. For all ages, aluminum sugar scoops or ice cream spades are durable (not cheap but last for years).

Water Play Tools

Big old clean paintbrush and bucket or can with handle to "paint" with water, outdoors. Small watering can. Florist's rubber sprayer (also a good bath toy). Small squares of old toweling or bits of sponges to wash dolls with. Little plastic cups to wash dolls' hair with.

Boxes, Boxes

See that nails do not stick out. Big boxes to climb on and get into. Packing boxes, refrigerator boxes, movers' garment boxes, large Fudgsicle cartons that ice cream manufacturers give away. Boxes, wood or cardboard, to make playhouses, stoves, puppet theaters, sinks. Hat-boxes to decorate, to store things in, to make little rooms or theaters from (part of one side cut away). Gallon and five-gallon round ice cream cartons (given away by ice cream places) to store things, to decorate, to make wastebaskets. Shallow wooden boxes or old bureau drawers or table drawers to put wheels on (or casters or domes) to use to store toys in and as trucks and trains. (Attach together with cup hook on one and screw eye on the other. Roll under bed when not in use.) Little boxes for treasures. Cigar boxes given away by pipe and tobacco shops. Empty cottage cheese cartons with lids.

Flashlight

Ticket Punch (paper punch)

Toothpicks (colored and plain)

Play Dough

> A few drops of food color in 2 cups water, 2 cups flour, 1 cup salt, ½ cup cornstarch, 2 tablespoons vegetable oil, 1 tablespoon powdered alum. Cook over medium heat until thick. Knead. Store in refrigerator.

Assorted Empty Cans

> Clean, no sharp edges, and labels taken off. Small sandbox toys for making cakes, scooping, and molding sand. (Also use old muffin tins, cake molds, and so on.) As planters (holes punched in bottom), as nesting toys, as containers of all kinds.

	SUGGESTED LEARNING TOYS	
Age	*Toy*	*Maker*
(months)		
6–24	Tote 'n Play	Playskool
6–36	Busy Poppin' Pals	Gabriel
	Teddy Bear Shape Sorter	Playskool
	Kiddie Links	Playskool
	Clown Stack	Playskool
12–36	Kitty in the Kegs	Gabriel
	Nuts 'n' Bolts	Gabriel
12–48	Pegboard (Little-Big)	Lauri
	Pegboard (Large)	Lauri
	Peg Log	Lauri
	Peg People	Lauri

Age	Toy	Maker
	Bristle Blocks, 64 pcs.	Playskool
	Wood Blocks	Playskool
	Wood Beads	Playskool
18–36	Jr. Fit-A-Space	Lauri
	Fix-A-Group	Lauri
	Towerifics (building toys)	James
18–48	Familiar Things	Lauri
(years)		
2–4	Keys of Learning	Gabriel
	Lacing Shapes	Lauri
3–5	Beads & Baubles	Lauri
	Fit-A-Size	Lauri
	Fit-A-Space	Lauri
	Play Tiles	Playskool
	Playskool Match-ups	Playskool
	Colors & Things	Playskool
	Animal Homes	Playskool
	Go-Togethers	Playskool
	Words to Spell	Playskool
	Picture ABCs	Playskool
	Count from 1 to 24	Playskool
3–6	Ji-Gan-Tiks, 31 pcs.	James
	Ji-Gan-Tiks, 43 pcs.	James
	Dominos	Benny & Smith
	Objects	Benny & Smith
	Animals	Benny & Smith
	Numbers	Benny & Smith
3–7	Numbers (1–10)	Lauri
	Lower (or) Upper ABC	Lauri
3–10	Close-up Cricket	Gabriel
	Judy Clock (wooden)	Judy
	Lauri Clock (tactile)	Lauri
4–7	Schoolhouse Playboards	Benny & Smith
	Letters/Sounds	Benny & Smith
	Counting Numbers	Benny & Smith
	Fun Boxes (puzzles)	Benny & Smith
	Find & Read	Benny & Smith

Age	Toy	Maker
	Spelling Words	Benny & Smith
4–10	Telling Time Game	Benny & Smith
	Making Change Game	Benny & Smith
	Ring-a-Majigs, 32 pcs.	James
	Ring-a-Majigs, 130 pcs.	James
	Drawing Steps	Crayola
	Hip-Opposites	Games/Learn Inc.
	Roh-The-Python	Games/Learn Inc.
	Number Plaques	Lauri

GAMES THAT TEACH READING READINESS SKILLS

Memory	Lord of the Rings
Doghouse	Jack in the Beanstalk
Cluster Puzzles	Dig It
Your America	Perfection
See the USA	Superfection
Trac 4	Challenge Perfection
Mad Libs	Whatchamacallit
Mug Shots	Password
Concentration	The Economy Game
Happy Day Solitaire	Waterworks

Surviving as a Volunteer

Womanpower has been the prime mover for social betterment in our country since its beginning. These years you spend at home to nurture your family can bring the expansion of mind and experience and enable you to make a worthy contribution to the community.

As a volunteer, you can choose how much time you can give and where you would like to put your efforts.

All churches and synagogues are dependent on committed volunteers to carry the teaching responsibilities at all levels. You can learn a lot about your own children while working with other children and other parents.

All our social agencies rely heavily on volunteers to carry out their programs—Cub Scouts, Girl Scouts, Campfire Girls, 4-H, Mental Health, and Family Services groups, YWCA, YMCA, to name a few.

The schools need parent volunteers for PTA, room mothers, teachers' aides. Any child benefits if his mother knows his teachers personally. Many of the special education programs need volunteer helpers. Hospitals and nursing homes need volunteers for all kinds of jobs.

If you choose to give your time to one of these needs or to anything that expands your interests and talents on a once-a-week basis, you will find life more exciting and enjoy your children more because you are doing something for yourself. Working with other adults on a regular basis relieves the feeling of being trapped by housework and children.

These experiences can lead to a part-time or full-time job when your children are older. They prepare you to challenge the empty-nest syndrome later on, for someday your children *will* leave, impossible as that may seem at this point in your life.

Be a Child Advocate

Children cannot speak for themselves, so concerned adults need to speak for them.

Knowing that the quality of life in the early years determines the quality of life later on, we in America need to value our children more and work for quick action to meet these needs.

THE NEED FOR REQUIRED COURSES ON HUMAN RELATIONSHIPS AND PARENTING IN EVERY JUNIOR AND SENIOR HIGH SCHOOL

Every state requires training to drive a car but not preparation to rear a child. Since 1975 a million teenagers have become pregnant every year—50 percent of them conceive out of wedlock; about 600,000 (97 percent of those who deliver) keep their babies; about 400,000 have abortions. In 1980 about 44 percent were unwed and under fifteen.

THE NEED FOR GOOD PARENTING TRAINING FOR PARENTS OF ALL AGES

Parents should be responsible for sending the schools a child who is physically, emotionally, and intellectually ready to learn. In 1980 there were 5 million neglected and abused children referred to family service agencies.

THE NEED TO PROVIDE QUALITY DAY CARE FOR PRESCHOOLERS

In 1980 more than half the mothers in the U.S. worked outside the home. There were 7.5 million children under thirteen who needed day care, but places for only 3.5 million in licensed facilities, so 4 million children were cared for by relatives, neighbors, or older children who were home alone.

THE NEED FOR SPECIAL TRAINING FOR ALL PERSONS WHO ARE ENTRUSTED WITH THE CARE OF OUR YOUNG CHILDREN

Good quality day care could provide a quality foundation for life.

We as a society must assume the responsibility for the welfare of our young children (as we do for our school-age children) so we can begin to reduce the many problems in our schools and communities.

The cost of these services would be no more than we are now spending on remedial programs, alternative schools, mental and social services, and welfare. We need *prevention* programs to replace *salvage* programs.

Skilled parenting, an honorable and rewarding endeavor, benefits the child, the mother, the father, and society. Anything less compounds the problems.

Picture Books for Young Children

Birth to Two Years

(Most of these books come in paperback editions)

Boynton, Sandra, *Moo Baa La La La.*

Hoban, Tana, *What Is It?*

Kelley, True, *Look, Baby! Listen, Baby! Do, Baby!*

Kunhardt, Dorothy, *Pat the Bunny.*

Mayer, Mercer, *Just a Snowy Day.*

Wells, Rosemary, *Max's New Suit.*

Two Years and Up

Ahlberg, Janet and Allen, *Jolly Postman.*

Anglund, Joan W., *The Brave Cowboy.*

Bang, Molly, *Ten, Nine, Eight.*

Brett, Jan, *Annie And The Wild Animals.*

Brooke, L. Leslie, *Johnny Crow's Garden.*

Brown, Margaret Wise, *Goodnight Moon.*

Burton, Virginia Lee, *Mike Mulligan and His Steam Shovel.*

Carle, Eric, *The Very Busy Spider.*

Dennis, Wesley, *Flip.*

De Regniers, Beatrice S., *May I Bring a Friend?*

Ehlert, Lois, *Planting A Rainbow.*

Ets, Marie E., *Play With Me.*

Flack, Marjorie, *Angus and the Cat.*

———, *Ask Mister Bear.*

———, *Story About Ping.*

Gag, Wanda, *Millions Of Cats.*

Gramatky, Hardie, *Little Toot.*

Hague, Kathleen, *Alphabears: An ABC Book.*

Handford, Martin, *Where's Waldo?*

Hoban, Russell, *Bedtime For Frances.*

Hughes, Shirley, *Bathwater's Hot.*

Johnson, Crockett, *A Picture For Harold's Room.*

Keats, Ezra Jack, *The Snowy Day.*

Krauss, Ruth, *A Hole Is To Dig.*

Leaf, Munroe, *Story of Ferdinand.*

Lopshire, Robert, *Put Me In The Zoo.*

McCloskey, Robert, *Blueberries For Sal.*

McCloskey, Robert, *Make Way For Ducklings.*

———, *Lentil.*

Potter, Beatrix, *The Tale Of Peter Rabbit.*

———, *The Tale Of Squirrel Nutkin.*

Raffi Songs to Read, *The Wheels On The Bus.*

Rey, Hans A., *Curious George.*

Scarry, Richard, *Richard Scarry's Cars And Trucks And Things That Go.*

Sendak, Maurice, *Where The Wild Things Are.*

Seuss, Dr., *And To Think That I Saw It On Mulberry Street.*

———, *Horton Hatches The Egg.*

Talbott, Hudson, *We're Back! A Dinosaur's Story.*

Helpful Books for Further Reading

Bettelheim, Bruno, *Uses of Enchantment.*
Explains the meaning and importance of Fairy Tales.

Bradshaw, John, *Bradshaw on: the Family.*
Understanding the dysfunctional family.

Brazelton, Berry, *Infants and Mothers.*
Discusses differences in development.

_____ , *Toddlers and Parents.*
Peaceful existence with toddlers.

Briggs, Dorothy C., *Your Child's Self Esteem, the Key to His Life.* A must for understanding young children, covers middle and adolescent child.

Cherry, Clare, *Please Don't Sit on the Kids.*
Alternatives to punitive punishment.

_____ , *Think of Something Quiet.*
Keeping peace the quiet way.

Davis, Adelle/Dr. Parker, *Let's Have Healthy Children.*
The classic on nutrition and how to keep everybody healthy and happy.

Dodson, Fitzhugh, *How to Parent.*
This covers the subject in clear detail. The school readiness helps include toys, records and books for each age.

———— , *How to Father.*
My favorite book for fathers, with a gold mine of information for mothers, too. Includes middle and older child.

Spock, Benjamin, *Baby and Child Care.*
The most widely published and complete manual on child care.

White, Burton L., *The First Three Years of Life.*
New research on the vital importance of the early years and guidelines for healthy growth and development.